# DATE

## Dundrum Adult Training and Education

*Celebrating 30 Years*

# DATE

## Dundrum Adult Training and Education

### *Celebrating 30 Years*

EDITED BY LIAM BANE

CARROWMORE

First published 2015

Carrowmore
50 City Quay
Dublin 2
Ireland
www. carrowmore.ie

British Library Cataloguing in Publication Data.
A catalogue record for this book is available from the British Library.

ISBN 978 0 9931716 0 4

Typeset in Garamond 12/15pt
Printed in Ireland

'What occurred to me when you made a very brief speech about the background of the establishment of DATE is that you have a story here that must be told, and must be told while there are those of you here who have been here from the beginning. And I have met founder members, I've met teachers and I've met students who have been here from the beginning and all of you have a contribution to make to that story. So if there is one thing I would urge you to do it is – pull that story together and tell it in permanent form …

It would be wonderful if you could make a commitment to drawing it together as a very interesting story of how you empowered yourselves here, how you went about it, the difficulties and also the achievements and I think that it's a very worthwhile and very interesting story and I think it's a story that would be widely read in Dundrum and the surrounding area because of the number of students who have come here, because of the impact you have made on the lives of very many people.'

(Extract from the address of President Mary Robinson on the occasion of her visit to Dundrum in 1994 to mark the tenth anniversary of DATE.)

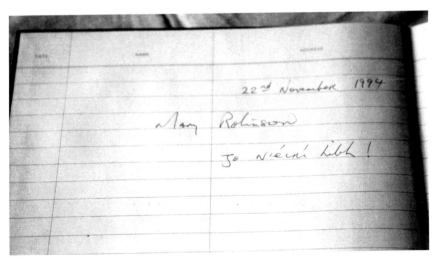

President Mary Robinson's signature

# Contents

# Remembering DATE through the Years

**Mary Elliott** is a founder member of the DATE committee. She was an elected member of Dublin County Council. Later she was chairperson of Dún Laoghaire Rathdown County Council and also served as chairperson of County Dublin Vocational Education Committee. Mary has always listed the promotion of adult education as a top priority.

**Teresa O'Neill**, also a founder member of DATE, is a former chairperson of the committee and has served DATE faithfully for over thirty years.

**Mary Cummins**, founder member and former chairperson of DATE, has also done sterling work in the promotion of the adult education service. She was for many years chairperson of the Adult Community Education Network (ACE) and a representative of the voluntary groups on the Co. Dublin VEC Adult Education Board.

Here Mary Cummins offers what is, in effect, a brief history of DATE over the years 1984–2014.

## 'The past is a foreign country,' wrote author L. P. Hartley, 'they do things differently there.'

A time traveller from today revisiting Ireland in the early 1980s could be forgiven for thinking he was in a different country. Ireland was traditional, conservative and set in its thinking and in its customs. At that time, most married women worked 'within the home'. Our position was protected by the constitution and was sacrosanct. We were told frequently by both the Church and the State that ours was the most important work – bringing up the nation's children for God and country.

Times were changing though – slowly but surely and irrevocably. The first Minister for Women's Affairs had been appointed. Nuala Fennell had many objectives and one was to get women out of the home and into the workforce. This was controversial at the time, not least among women themselves. Many felt it undervalued their work and undermined their status in the community. Many others could not wait to get back into the workplace. All of us felt a vague longing for something more.

When a poster was put up in Dundrum Post Office it caught our attention. The poster read, 'Are you interested in becoming involved in daytime classes with crèche facilities? Come to a public meeting in Dundrum.' It was a wet grey day in April 1984 and the venue for the meeting was down a flight of kamikaze stairs leading to the hall under the church. The concrete steps were wet and the metal handrail was slimy from the rain. Not a place to bring a child in a buggy. However, with the help of my friend, Joan Godkin, mother and child (and buggy) got safely down.

There was a sizeable crowd of people there – all women. We presumed they were there for the same reasons as we were – to escape domesticity for a while and to stop our brains from slowly ossifying. A dark-haired young woman called Mary McCarthy was speaking. She wanted to bring adult and 'second-chance' education into the local community in partnership with Co. Dublin VEC. Mary felt that everyone should be able to access education at a reasonable cost, close to home. Crèche facilities were a must. This was also one of Nuala Fennell's objectives and it sounded fine to us. Our attitude was, 'Let us know when and where the classes will be starting and we'll be there.' The meeting was also addressed by Liam Bane and Fred Goulding, Adult Education Organisers. Then somebody passed round a piece of paper and we wrote down our details. We also specified which subjects we were most interested in. The meeting ended and the crowd began to filter out of the hall.

Joan and I hung back to let everyone go ahead. Mary McCarthy approached us looking for volunteers for a committee. I protested that I could not join. 'You can found a crèche,' said Mary. Joan's protests were likewise dismissed. We were 'roped in as volunteers', Joan later wrote. Mary Elliott reported a similar experience. Shortly afterwards, we attended our first meeting in Dundrum House. A pub was certainly not an ideal venue. Creeping in that first morning, some of us pushing prams, we tried to look as inconspicuous as possible. Some of the pub 'regulars' looked a bit startled at this sudden influx of women but we pretended not to notice. Ordering tea and coffee all round, we commandeered the largest table and we were ready to proceed. Immediately Mary McCarthy named the officers of the new committee. Mary Elliott found that she had been appointed secretary to the as yet unnamed group. Joan Godkin was treasurer and Mary McCarthy was the chairperson. I was still the designated crèche founder. Mary Elliott voiced all of our thoughts when she said, 'What have we let ourselves in for?'

There were regular furtive meetings of the committee in the pub after that. Mary McCarthy introduced us to adult education. Groups like us were setting up all over the country. New and more 'student-friendly' methods of learning that were more appropriate to adults would be used. We were also introduced to the concept of Lifelong Learning. The business side of our new endeavour was not neglected either. A note in the minutes recalls that a collection of £5 each from all those present was taken up at the meeting on 12 June 1984 and used to open a bank account. Did we ever get it back? We cannot remember!

One morning we were waiting for our scheduled committee meeting to begin. Mary McCarthy was late, which was unlike her. Then she rang the pub to say that she was very unwell and could not attend the meeting. She urged us, most earnestly, to continue with the project. There was a worried discussion among the fledgling committee about how we should proceed. Mary had been our leader. Pamela Uhlemann was present at this meeting, by my request. We hoped she would run the crèche for us. She was promptly 'volunteered' to take on the chairpersonship and so found herself appointed both chair and crèche leader at the same time. Mary McCarthy's departure left us in another quandary. She was the sole contact person with the VEC's Adult Education Organiser, Liam Bane.

Finally, at summer's end, we decided that it was imperative to get in touch with Mr Bane. A delegation was dispatched to find him. When he was found, we discovered that he had spent the summer finding premises, planning a brochure and engaging tutors to teach the subjects on that brochure. He had put his trust in a group of strangers from a public meeting and they, in turn, had put their trust in him. It boded well for the future.

## Dundrum Adult Education Centre
### (Old Taney School, Eglinton Terrace)

Yes! This was our address. We actually had an address. From the idea of an adult education centre being mooted in April to its realisation in early September, our work and commitment had resulted in an amazing achievement. Of course, the groundwork had been laid over many months before the public meeting in Dundrum by Mary McCarthy and her associates, Jo Whelan and Elizabeth Kehoe. Both Jo and Elizabeth were unfortunately unable to join Dundrum Adult Education Centre due to work commitments.

Enrolling day was upon us, the beginning of our adventure. We were all there – the 'voluntary' committee made up of the two Kathleens (Berrigan and Walker), the three Marys (McCarthy, Elliott

First Annual General Meeting D.A.T.E.
25ª June 1985    U.E.C.

Present:  Pamela Uhleman, Mary Elliott, Joan Godkin,
Mary Cummins, Olive Carroll, Liam Bane
Ann Mc Connell, Teresa O'Neill, John O'Callega
- Chris Hickey.

Minutes read by Mary Elliott
Chairman's Report given by Pamela Uhlemann
Pamela read section from Liam's book.
Constitution read by Mary Elliott
Pamela proposed amendment to constitution:
D.A.T.E be non sectarian and non political
How to become member D.A.T-E ??
Additions to constitution.
Mary Cummins to word how to become member.
~~The~~ It was proposed that changes in constitution
can only be made at A.G.M.

Coffee Break 11.A.m.

Another amendment to constitution:
Committee elected at AGM if 12 quota present.
Committee decisions of absent Committee members
of re opt on Committee.
Chris was proposed and seconded on Committee

The first AGM, 25 June 1985

and Cummins), Joan Godkin, Teresa O'Neill, Catherine O'Reilly,
Pamela Uhlemann (our chairperson) and our Adult Education
Organiser, Liam Bane. We were offering fourteen classes over three
days. There would be two yoga classes, Basic English and French on
Mondays. We offered Basic Maths, Crafts and Life Skills (Eastern

Pamela Uhlemann and Mary Cummins

Health Board) on Tuesdays. There were two computer classes, Basic Irish and Active Retirement (EHB) on Thursdays. In addition, we were offering Leaving Cert. English and Maths on Monday and Thursday at a cost of £25 for twenty weeks. Both EHB classes cost £5 each and all others £15 per term with reduced prices for senior citizens. We had, we hoped, a winning formula for starting an adult education centre. Take one male Adult Education Organiser, who undoubtedly knew what he was doing, add eight housewives, one male and six female teachers, and one qualified crèche person, mix with the main ingredient – the students – and hope for the best.

Sitting behind the desks with the dreaded official receipt books at the ready, we felt a mixture of excitement and apprehension.

The doors opened and people of all ages came in: mothers with pushchairs, the middle-aged and retired people. There were even some men. It seemed natural and normal to us to welcome them as students.

'Come one – come all'. As people approached us at the tables, we tried to look as competent and 'used to this kind of thing' as we could. An abiding memory of them is how hesitant and apologetic some of them were.

'I might be too old.'

'I left school at fourteen – will I be able for the classes?'

'I'm not the most academic but I want to use my brain.'

'I have always wanted to try my hand at the Leaving Cert.'

'It won't be like school, will it?'

Our hearts went out to them. We reassured them as best we could. 'This is about adult education. It is designed for adults. You'll be fine.'

We worked away at enrolling, trying very hard to get everything right. At the end of that first day the money was accurate and the receipts were very nearly perfect. We breathed a collective sigh of relief.


## The Old Taney School

The adventure began in earnest when we opened our doors to begin classes in the old Taney National School. Everything seemed to slot into place so easily. The students went into classes where the teachers awaited them and the learning began. There was an incredible atmosphere from the beginning. The tutors were delighted to be teaching adults, who, unlike schoolchildren, were there because they had chosen to be there. The students came out of the classes relaxed, interested and pleased that this experience was so unlike their previous classroom experiences. The essential business of the learning dialogue had begun. Pamela and Ann McConnell were looking after the children in the crèche. Ann had come to help Pamela but loved the 'buzz' of the classes and she quickly joined the committee.

Taney School was a picturesque old place but normally used only for Scout meetings or jumble sales. Teresa O'Neill puts the task the committee faced very succinctly, 'Little did we realise what was ahead of us. The premises were not the best, to put it mildly. Hard work was the name of the game. Furniture had to be moved, cleaning had to be done, heating had to be looked after and the cup of tea was a must.' The committee also had the task of opening and closing the premises, passing the key to the person on duty that day. The person on duty assisted the 'computer man' to bring the large monitors in and out of the building and anything else that needed to be done.

As autumn progressed, we found we had a problem with the premises. They were cold, cold like we had never felt before. The main hall and the largest classroom were heated by gas wall heaters. These hissed and spluttered away merrily when 50p coins were fed into the meter. No one noticed them until they began to fizzle out. There would be a pounding of feet across the wooden floor and then the reassuring clunk as a committee member dropped 50p into the meter and the hissing recommenced. We were very economical with our 50p coins. Mary Elliott remembers being on duty on cold winter mornings and having to rush to the shop for change. It was still cold though and Liam got us 'Supersers' for the other rooms. They were ever so slightly old and decrepit. Liam discovered a rare gift for getting those accursed things to work. There was a big 'to-do' when he was not there. The conveniences were inconvenient also (they were child-sized) and only accessible through an external courtyard.

Despite all of these drawbacks, adult learners returned in increased numbers in spring 1985. Could it be that the learning environment was more important than the physical environment?

The crèche was a major responsibility and concern for the committee. 'No crèche – no classes' was a popular mantra among adult education groups at this time. The VEC did not have crèche provision within its brief, so it fell to the committee to provide and fund the crèche. We had thought that it could be self-financing but the amount we made from crèche fees only paid for the insurance. We began a series of information mornings, complete with cake sales, to raise funds. We used the 'coffee money' and ran some classes of our own to help as well.

In March 1985, we held our first open day. Nuala Fennell attended in her capacity as Minister for Women's Affairs. She brought a film crew from RTÉ with her. We were thrilled to see it on television that night although it was only a very brief report. Minister Fennell made a speech praising our work. She was particularly impressed with the crèche provision and her department gave us a grant of £500 towards its upkeep. This enabled us to pay 'back wages' to the crèche staff and get some additional equipment for the children.

Premises were another concern. Our stay in Taney was tenuous at best. We were only there on a 'term-to-term' basis. In the meantime, we pursued every county councillor, every TD, all VEC personnel and any other person perceived by us to have any influence whatsoever in our quest for premises. We usually hunted in pairs or trios. At one stage, we were intent on purchasing Shamrock House near the Garda station on the Kilmacud Road. We went so far as to have the local auctioneers evaluate it. We also asked other groups in the area to support us by pledging to use it as well. This turned out to be too ambitious a project even for us. Undeterred, we returned with increased vigour to pursuing the politicians and the VEC personnel.

## DATE – Dundrum Adult Training and Education

In September 1986, we entered a whole new phase in the ongoing development of what was now DATE.

The VEC gave us a prefab solely for our use on the grounds of the College of Commerce. The location was perfect. It was right in the middle of Dundrum, off Main Street, opposite the shopping centre and near the church and the library. We were delighted with it, despite knowing that it would not be a permanent home for us, given our rate of growth. Pamela had left DATE to pursue her career and Ann had taken over as chair. I had taken over Ann's old job as vice chair. Kathleen Walker left in 1985 to assist her daughter in a business enterprise. Mary Elliott was now a county councillor and had performed her first official duty for us when she presented prizes to our Leaving Certificate graduates. John O'Callaghan had joined the committee in 1985 from the Active Retirement class and described himself as our 'token man'. Olive Carroll had also joined us in 1985 and Kay Bailey joined us in 1986. With Pamela's departure, we needed a suitably qualified person to run the crèche and to meet the insurance criteria. We advertised in the papers and subsequently appointed Eilish Kavanagh, a qualified Montessori teacher.

We set up the all-important tea and coffee table in the lobby of the prefab opposite the front door and we were ready for business. We were now offering twenty-eight separate classes, including a certificate in Counselling and a Social Studies class from Maynooth. Economics and History had been added to the Leaving Cert. subjects. We easily filled all the classes. This was a whole new world for the committee. With an excellent caretaker in Tom Newman and later in Paddy Brett, our furniture-shifting and heating-repair needs were sorted. Life became easier for the committee and we had more fun. Although we had officers on the committee, we tried to have a 'round table' approach where everyone had a role to play. The lines were already blurred between the AEO, the committee and the teachers. We had held planning meetings in Taney where it was obvious that everyone – teachers, committee and AEO – were dedicated to making DATE a haven for all learners, including ourselves. We rediscovered our identities. We were Ann or Joan or Teresa or Mary, our true selves. With the encouraging and nurturing environment that was created, I think we became our best selves.

There was a great deal of activity in adult education at that time and we sent representatives to all adult education events. Many aspiring groups approached Liam wishing to set up adult education centres. Liam usually brought two or three different people to each meeting, adding 'chauffeur' to his other duties. We went to Rathfarnham, to Ballyboden, to Monkstown, to name a few. The farthest flung of these was a group from Galway. They had visited us in Taney and now invited us to a public meeting in Galway on 9 June 1986. Liam brought Ann, Olive, John and me over for the day. There was a fair-sized crowd gathered in a community hall. Ann was a good speaker by now. At the end of every speech, she always courteously asked me if I had anything to add. Smugly, I always replied that she had covered everything. This time, however, I was asked specific questions about setting up a crèche and was forced to speak. I discovered that the sky did not fall down and I got through it. Joan's minutes of that day record that our group was invited to join the local group for lunch to continue the discussions. The Galway group started classes that September.

By 1987 we were looking for more space. One of our classrooms in the prefab had been taken away from us and another had been divided in two. While most of us were upset by this, it brought one benefit: Maura Murphy, our founding teacher, moved into one half of the divided room and found her spiritual home. 10a was to be her sanctuary. She taught all her beloved classes there for the twenty years we used the prefab. We moved some classes into Holy Cross National School. This was a golden time in DATE, despite the fact that we had to work much harder to manage two venues. Somehow we took it in our stride. Teresa again puts it very well, 'The committee was so energetic and enthusiastic in those good old days that nothing would come in our way from keeping the classes going.'

Our meetings were held in the College of Commerce in the evenings and we got into the habit of going back down to our 'alma mater', Dundrum House, afterwards. We were back to our tea and coffee days and with John and Liam's full participation we discussed every subject under the sun. We cannot now remember much about the discussions but the laughter and the fun resonate with us still.

Mary McCarthy had always maintained her interest in DATE. She had attended meetings and classes on and off as her health permitted. In 1987 we received the terrible news that she had passed away. She was only thirty-nine years of age. It is fair to say that without her vision and her determination DATE would never have come into being. Mary was proof that one person with a dream can make a difference to so many lives. I hope she realised how much she had accomplished in her short life and how much she meant to us.

The years 1988 and 1989 saw us still expanding. We had sixty-five separate classes. We met the best writers in Ireland – John McGahern,

James Plunkett, Eavan Boland, Kate Cruise O'Brien and others – when they attended the Writers' Workshop. We sold out our first cultural event, 'An Evening with Brendan Kennelly'.

Meanwhile, back in Holy Cross, the work was relentless. We were lucky enough to have two new committee members, Mary O'Brien and Jo Pakenham. The tea room was always full. We had huge numbers coming in and, from the practical housekeeping end of things, we were hard pressed to keep the hot water, the milk and the biscuits flowing. We never seemed to have enough cups either and spent much of our time washing up. Furniture arranging was still a major part of the work. The rooms had to be set up every day. We had set our hopes for more permanent accommodation on acquiring empty rooms in Holy Cross School. In March 1990, the then Minister for Education Mary O'Rourke visited us. The minister was very sympathetic and promised to investigate the situation for us. But the rooms remained empty.

Everything proceeded normally during the spring term of 1990. As in previous years, student enrolments had increased. Our annual open day was a great success and we 'informed' all the local politicians about our ongoing plight regarding premises. If they looked slightly glassy-eyed, who could blame them? In August, Ann rang to say that she had taken ill during a shopping trip. Unfortunately, it turned out to be a much more serious matter and Ann had to have an operation. She appeared to recover well and was in daily touch with me about every aspect of DATE. It frustrated her a great deal that she could not be there in the middle of everything.

In 1991 someone – I think it was Liam – came up with the idea of a cultural week as Dublin was the 1991 European City of Culture. We decided it should coincide with our open day. We were planning for weeks in advance. We had been joined for the autumn in 1990 by Marguerite Thornton and Ann O Briain and we were very glad of the extra help.

We held the Open Day on Tuesday 23 April as usual. That evening we held a major Art Exhibition in Dundrum College on Sydenham Road. Prizes were presented for the various categories and Marguerite arranged for the artist Robert Ballagh to present them. On the Wednesday we hosted a Writers' Evening in Ballinteer House and Mary Elliott engaged the author Patricia Scanlon to present the prizes. The following day there was a theatrical performance by the Balally Players and the actor Brendan Cauldwell. Liam borrowed a stage from St Attracta's School for the occasion. And on the Friday we had a ceili in Ballinteer House. By the end of the week, we were all exhausted. We swore off 'culture' for the foreseeable future, if not forever.

On 5 September that year, Ann attended a committee meeting and we dared to hope that she was getting better. We enrolled 1,220 students in seventy classes that term and morale was high. On New Year's Eve, we heard the devastating news that Ann had died. She was forty-six years old. A bright light had been extinguished from our lives forever. She brought joy and laughter, friendship and goodness into everything she did. Ann had given us our mantra for DATE, 'Nobody should leave this place (DATE) feeling less of a person than when they came here.'

The cycle continued much as it had over the previous years. We held the planning meeting, we worked on our brochure, we enrolled for the term and we made tea and coffee. Life went on, although it would never be quite the same again. We were at full stretch. We could not expand any further. We had eight or nine rooms in Holy Cross, we had four rooms in the prefab and we had now added the Dom Marmion Centre to our portfolio. Enrolling had become a major operation and we put a lot of effort into ensuring the safety and welfare of our students. Long queues would form early in the morning and snake through the corridors of the little building, often even extending outside. We tried to process the new students with as much expediency and friendliness as possible. We were assisted by the teachers and a group of helpers. We had gained two new committee members, Maureen Flynn and Dolores Byrne, and we were, as usual, very glad of the help they gave us. Around this time, Finn Doyle joined our group as a helper, and would later become a committee member. Finn loved making tea and coffee for the students and turned the task into a gracious ceremony. She was with us until after her ninetieth birthday. Eventually, she found it too tiring and stopped coming. The students still remember her.

## A Visit from the President

The day was progressing as usual at the tea table in the prefab. One of the students asked to speak to me privately. She asked if DATE would be interested in having the presidential candidate Mary Robinson make a visit to DATE. I thought it was a great idea but said that I would have to consult with the committee. The committee was very enthusiastic but we felt that the other presidential candidates should also be asked, so we invited both Brian Lenihan and Austin Curry. Mary Robinson arrived to see us one bright morning. We brought her to see Holy Cross and the prefab. She was courteous and interested and very enthusiastic about the work we were doing.

As we approached the tenth anniversary of DATE in 1994, we decided to write to Mary Robinson, now president, to see if she would visit us again. To our surprise and delight she agreed to come. We prepared assiduously for the great occasion. We opted for an open day format with stands representing all, or most, subjects. Each tutor would 'man' their own stand, accompanied by a student representative. It was a mammoth task. Liam worked away steadily with us as usual and we all studied the protocol. We invited Mary McCarthy's husband as well as Ann McConnell's family and Kathleen Walker and Kathleen Berrigan from the original 'volunteers'. The committee and special guests would be presented to the president in the hallway, the president would then be escorted around the exhibition and finally there would be speeches. We submitted all this information and the list of names in good time. We received word back that all was well.

The stately old car swept into the grounds with the flags flying. Mary Elliott and I greeted the president and her aide-de-camp and led them to the prefab. Mary Robinson took great care to greet each individual personally. We walked around the exhibition, stopping at every stand.

The president is greeted by Mary Elliott, Mary Cummins, Liam Bane and Teresa O'Neill

SOUTHNEWS EXPRESS

● *President Mary Robinson meets with Trish O'Rourke and baby Kate in Dundrum last week.*

Dundrum Adult Training and Education Centre (DATE) last week celebrated its 10th birthday and members were joined at the party in the College of Commerce, Dundrum, by the President Mrs. Mary Robinson.

DATE, the largest education operation of its kind in the country, is run by a local voluntary committee and promotes daytime education for adults in the greater Dundrum area.

In 1984 DATE had 12 classes and 180 students, today it caters for 1,200 students attending 78 classes five mornings a week.

"Students here study the Junior and Leaving Certificate Courses, for diploma's from Maynooth and UCD, and other subjects including yoga, woodwork and furniture restoration," Mary Cummins, DATE Chairperson told SouthNews. "The age groups vary enormously, we have people here ranging from 18 to 88, and they come from all over the city."

'President Mary Robinson meets with Trish O'Rourke and baby Kate in Dundrum last week'

The president and Teresa O'Neill

The president with Mary Cummins and Mary Elliott

Our caretaker, Tom Newman, presented the president with a beautiful wooden bowl he had crafted himself. Finally it was time for speeches. I gave a brief speech and then the president spoke. She said that from what she had seen and heard on her visit there was a book to be written about DATE and that this should be done while the founder committee members, Liam, the original teachers and students were around to tell the story. It has taken twenty years to fulfil her request.

That year Marguerite took over as chairperson and served a four-year term. The clientele in DATE was changing. The VEC colleges were now providing 'back-to-work' courses for adults and there were also jobs available for more mature people in the workforce. The number of students attending dropped but there was still plenty of work for the volunteers.

Mary Elliott had made adult education a priority in her career as a county councillor. In DATE she could be found making the tea or coffee or doing her stint at enrolling time like the rest of us. She had become a member of Co. Dublin VEC in 1991. She was the chairperson of the Ad Hoc Adult Education Board and I was privileged to represent the voluntary groups on this board. Mary was also the chairperson of the Education Board in 1995/96 when she made a keynote speech, launching a booklet on adult and community education. The significance that she attached to the work of DATE and the other voluntary groups is clear from the following quotation from that speech. 'The ethos of our groups in County Dublin is to meet the education needs of all students, fulfilling the needs of the whole community, ensuring equal rights of access for everyone whatever their age, gender, race, class, level of ability or disability.'

The cycle of DATE continued and Dolores Byrne took over as chairperson. About halfway through her tenure, we received news that we were to lose the Holy Cross premises because of heating problems. We now had seven or eight different venues for our classes and the committee was run ragged. Kay O'Reilly, who joined DATE during that time, found she was allocated to Airfield because she had a car and she rarely got to see any committee members. Eileen O'Brien and

Ann Brodie had also joined us on the committee by then. All of us only came together at committee meetings and we tried to catch up with family and other news then.

During this time we lost our dear committee colleagues Joan Godkin, Geraldine Whittaker and John O'Callaghan. Joan set the highest standards for herself but was most forgiving of the foibles of others. Liam said that Joan was always on the lookout for the 'lost lamb' to help and console. Geraldine was lively and outgoing and was taken in the prime of life, a young woman, wife and mother with lots of living still to do. John had been a staunch friend and ally to all of us and a founder member of DARA (Dundrum Active Retirement Association). His sense of humour and his laugh were infectious. They were all three a great loss and we missed them very much.

Geraldine Whittaker

Teresa took over as chairperson from Dolores and we continued as best we could. Jo Whelan, who had been one of people who called the public meeting that led to DATE, retired from work and joined the committee. Jo loved being a committee member and is currently the vice chairperson of DATE.

## Dundrum Town Centre

Kathleen Walker had re-joined the committee some years previously and her friend Maureen Nolan had joined with her. Both women were very active in areas of community service, including local radio and the residents' association. In fact, it was through the combined residents' associations that Kathleen heard news of a huge new shopping centre being proposed as part of a redevelopment in Dundrum. Some space was being allocated for voluntary and community groups and Kathleen urged us to write to the developers. We were surprised to receive a positive reply and so began a consultation process.

Co. Dublin VEC and DATE were represented by Mary Elliott and Liam Bane who attended innumerable meetings. When Liam retired, our new AEO, Patricia Doran, continued the process in partnership with Mary. Our partners in seeking accommodation were Dundrum Local Radio and the Citizens' Advice Bureau.

Finally we got the news for which we had waited over twenty years. Teresa's words say it all, 'After many years of hard work and many setbacks, thankfully they (Mary, Liam and Patricia) were successful in getting classroom space on the top floor of the new town centre. It was a great achievement and a wonderful day for DATE. We had premises of our own at last. We moved into our brand new premises in September 2006. We had a fine big tea room, six classrooms and an office. It has been great having most classes under the same roof which leads to a more friendly atmosphere all round. Our dream has come true.'

Ann Brodie was the chairperson who took us through the transition and into our new premises. We have thrived in Dundrum Town Centre where we have over a thousand students attending classes per term. We have a wonderful caretaker in Aiden who embodies the spirit and ethos of DATE, while Michelle, our secretary, is friendly and courteous to everyone. We have a large and enthusiastic committee to continue the good work of DATE. We have recruited Katherine Chandler, Felicity Fitzpatrick, Roisin Daly, Brenda McIntyre, Mary Sarsfield and, most recently, Catherine O'Brien.

For us 'old timers', it has been a marvellous adventure. We have participated in the birth and growth of one of the biggest adult education centres in the country. We have seen the life-changing effects it has had on people. We have met wonderful people who have enriched our lives and we have also learned a little along the way.

Some of our first tutors: (Standing) Eamon Cass, Valerie Coombes, Mary Purcell, Mairin Elliot; (Seated) Beatrice Stewart, Trish Haugh, Pauline Brady

# Recollection

**Marguerite Thornton**, member of the DATE committee and former chairperson.

I first became associated with DATE about twenty-six years ago. While collecting my children from school, I met Mary Cummins who invited me to go along to the prefabs in the College of Commerce in Dundrum. I went along and I can still remember the friendly faces at the all-important tea table. I was soon hooked and joined an art class. I somehow ended up on the committee a few months later. I didn't have any experience of committees but all that was needed was plenty of energy, a smile or two in the mornings for the students and the ability to move tables, chairs and heaters from one end of Dundrum to the other to all of our different venues. And, of course, I knew how to make tea. So my journey into the land of lifelong learning began.

Over the years, committee members have come and gone, including some of our best friends who passed away far too early. But the members of DATE have always been so supportive of each other as life changed and evolved within the group and within our families. This support, encouragement and friendliness have also always been there for our students, many of whom are still coming along to various classes after all these years.

In 2007, shortly after we moved into the Adult Education Centre in DTC, I started part-time work in the Literacy Office of the local VEC. I know that it was my involvement with DATE that gave me the confidence to apply for the position. I love my work in this sector as I am still involved with people who have come to us to improve their literacy and numeracy skills.

My life has been intertwined with DATE for many years now and my grandson Ben even remembers when I used to bring him to the DATE crèche when I was on duty there. My years of working with adults in DATE have shown me that lifelong learning is so important in every way. It doesn't have to be academically based, with certificates and diplomas. The greatest achievement is the coming together of people of all ages and abilities to learn and develop. I hope DATE, like the learning it promotes, is lifelong and goes on and on for many years to come.

# DATE – An Adventure in Adult Education

**Liam Bane** was appointed Adult Education Organiser for the South Co. Dublin area in 1980 and was involved in the establishment of the first programme of daytime classes for adults in 1984.

On a cold damp April morning, I made my way to the hall under the Catholic church in Dundrum, Dublin 14. I was going to attend a public meeting which had been called with a view to assessing the level of interest in starting a programme of daytime classes for adults. This was in 1984, four years since I had been appointed to the post of Adult Education Organiser by Co. Dublin Vocational Committee with the task of establishing an education service geared to meeting the various educational needs of adults in a particular area of South County Dublin. But these too were recessionary times and while, as organisers, we had been given the task, we had not been granted the necessary funding. In those early days, the only worthwhile initiative that I can recall was the establishment of an education programme at the Central Mental Hospital in Dundrum.

What was I like back then? Like some demented medieval knight wandering about the territory, seeking out windmills to tilt at – and if I found them, they would no doubt have been born again as adult education classrooms. I was like some ancient mariner, with an albatross firmly fixed about the neck, in search of an audience and inflicting the tale on any and all who would hear me out . But was anybody out there listening?

Then one morning I was visited in my office in the then College of Commerce by three women – Mary McCarthy, Josephine Whelan and Elizabeth Kehoe – who had just returned from a weekend seminar at the ICA headquarters in Temonfeckin organised by the Minister for Women's Affairs, the late Nuala Fennell. My visitors were anxious to return to education and raised the possibility of setting up daytime classes for adults. We talked, they offered help and we decided to call a public meeting.

It was a proposal that captured my interest and enthusiasm immediately. I recognised too that if it were to succeed, then it could only be achieved with the help and commitment of voluntary workers. Thus it was with a high degree of apprehension that I approached the church hall, thinking that even the weather had voted against. Imagine my surprise – and delight – to find a crowded hall. All women, of course, some with little children in buggies, but all with expectation and anticipation written all over their faces. Also present was Fred Goulding, a colleague who had just become involved in a similar project in Tallaght and who, just before the meeting ended, offered a very timely piece of advice: get the names of people who are willing to help NOW, before they leave the hall.

A page of a copybook was hastily procured and those wishing to become involved provided names, addresses and telephone numbers as well as listing subjects they wished to study.

In all, there were twenty-one signatories and there was quite a range of preferences expressed, from basic English to pre-university courses. And there were those who had stated simply 'any course'. Of these twenty-one signatories, seven were to be part of the founding committee, including Mary McCarthy, who was the first chairperson but who sadly did not live to see the realisation of her dream.

## Early Days

Thus a small seed had been planted but who could have foreseen the great big tree that would emerge from it? For my part, the immediate task was to find a suitable premises, which soon became any premises as school after school either could not or would not host daytime adult education classes. Adults, it would appear, were thought of like owls, fit for study at night only.

Finally a premises was found, a disused Church of Ireland building that had served as a primary school and, after negotiations with the amiable Rev. Desmond Sinnamon, the rent was agreed. The word 'suitable' does not really apply but it was nonetheless an adequate, if basic, place to make a start. I can still see the faces of the committee members as they surveyed the building for the first time – that vast empty space with its great high ceiling and its antiquated heating system that had to be coin fed regularly. It wasn't exactly an inviting or welcoming environment but at that point it was all that was available to us.

It was then that I learned that this was a committee different from others on which I had served. This was a committee of women who were determined to make things happen. It was fascinating to observe, to see how every problem was just another challenge for them, another obstacle to be overcome, one they would stay with until a solution was found. They took the concept and shaped and shook and moulded it. It didn't matter that these young mothers weren't familiar with Freire or Illich or hadn't yet taken the diploma in adult education theory. Because so much of their lives was spent coping and shaping and moulding and creating, they already had a very clear idea of what it was they wanted and how to make it happen. They knew they couldn't always expect the ideal solution but they always managed to come up with a pragmatic, practical one that would enable learning to take place.

No crèche, no class. No crèche? Alright then, let's run our own crèche. And who will mind the children? We, the committee members, will mind the children just as we will arrange the furniture every morning before and after class, just as we will sweep the floors, feed the meters, enrol the students, answer the phone. Anything else? Oh yes, very important, we will provide tea, coffee and biscuits at the break.

The next task was to decide on a curriculum. What classes should be offered? We were now in the realm of speculation and it was going to be a case of trial and error. For a start, we decided that there would be classes on three mornings a week – Monday, Tuesday and Thursday – and we drew up a programme that would offer different options, a mix of basic education, Leaving Cert. classes in English and Maths (or what we referred to as 'second-chance education'), health and fitness classes, and leisure time activities. We even offered a class called Computer Programming Basic Language Level 1, introducing adult students to the new technology that had announced its arrival and was to revolutionise our world over the following years. Peter arrived with his Apple Macs and somehow with an assortment of cables and plugs. Before long, six computers were wired up and running with places for twelve students – and how's this for value? An eight-week course for just £19!

There were twelve classes listed, including two run in co-operation with the Eastern Health Board, Lifeskills and Active Retirement. From that Active Retirement programme we recruited our first male committee member, John O'Callaghan, who fitted in beautifully and who sadly is no longer with us. There was also an Irish class and the tutor Mairin Elliott insisted on offering her time and talents free of charge.

September came, our first enrolment day arrived and the big doors of our quaint Victorian building were thrown open. Apprehension mounted as we awaited the arrival of our first adult students. We were not disappointed and from early morning, it was obvious that we were in business. An array of learners arrived, some quite confidently making their way to the appropriate table, others shy and uncertain and seeking advice. They were put at ease before long. And yes, there were some men amongst women.

From the very beginning of this adventure, the core principle had been established: this was a centre for adult learning where the learners' needs would be the most important consideration. This was going to be a place of learning where all voices would be heard, a place of learning where all would be included. All would be welcome as the inbuilt mother instinct of the committee members demanded that no one should feel an outsider, that all should be treated with respect. Thus it was that from those first very tentative steps, a special place was created where students felt safe and secure and, to my astonishment, they came day after day, some with buggies and snugly wrapped-up children. They sat huddled around tables, listening, questioning, discussing, supporting, advising, suggesting, sharing, learning and indeed laughing. Not even the sometimes arctic cold could drive them away.

## Those Prefab Days

At the end of our first year, May 1985, it was clear that we had struck a chord with the adult learning public and it was clear too from the students' consistent attendance that we had discovered a group of tutors who had instinctively grasped from the start the dynamic that was at work here, tutors who were able to identify the needs of the adult learner and who were able to respond to these needs and, more importantly, offer the support, empathy and affirmation so essential in these early stages. We had brought together people who were an integral part of a shared vision. We had an energetic, tireless committee; teachers, all employed on a part-time basis, who had won the trust of their students; and a large group of adults who were eager to learn and who were encouraged to leave behind any lingering fears and resentments they may have developed during previous negative educational experiences. It was wonderful to sense the warmth generated in this old cold draughty building by the eagerness and enthusiasm of both learners and teachers and the evident satisfaction they derived from this new experience.

It was clear also that there was now a need to expand if we were to respond to the growing demands. This was the start of what was to be an ongoing problem over the next twenty years – the quest for a suitable premises. In the spring term of 1986, in addition to the Taney premises, classes were offered in rented rooms in the Holy Cross primary school in Dundrum and in the autumn of that year, we were allocated four rooms in the College of Commerce, where we had the opportunity to develop a decent childcare facility with a qualified person in charge. We could now boldly say 'Crèche facilities available'. But what this moving and shifting entailed was the division of labour and more work for a hard-pressed committee. Rooms still had to be prepared, floors swept, tea and coffee facilities provided and a place to park the car had to be found outside the school grounds for all.

At this time too, it had become apparent that there was a coterie of students who saw their attendance at DATE classes as the gateway to further education. By way of response and, in collaboration with Maynooth College, we advertised our first diploma classes – Social Studies and a certificate in Counselling, which ran for twenty weeks. These were hugely popular and there were long queues for the counselling courses in particular. In that second year, we offered a programme of twenty-eight classes over two terms and the enrolment amounted to 595. A significant milestone was reached in 1989-90 when the total enrolments came to 1,121.

## Meeting New Demands

Every year, new classes were offered and as the numbers grew, the range and variety of options also expanded. For the health conscious, the yoga classes, which had been popular from the beginning, multiplied and other avenues were explored, such as Reflexology, Shiatsu and Natural Healing, Approaches to Holistic Living and even the exotic-sounding Introduction to Swedish Massage. There was a Liberal Studies course and Leadership Skills and Start Your Own Business. There were Media Studies and Classical Studies and an abundance of Art classes. For those who were determined to find answers, there was a course presented by a Jesuit priest called A Life Quest and there were courses for the philosophers and the psychologists. For those wishing to explore their origins, there was Anthropology and for those seeking more immediate and mundane answers, there was Law for the Lay Person. Language classes flourished – European languages of course and, for those who were interested, an Irish conversation class called *Bígí Ag Labhairt*. Interior decorating, a bridge club, cookery demos, 'Confidently Speaking', and those in search of academe could take diplomas in Environmental Studies, Psychology or Literature. For the students of ancient Greece and Rome, there was Classical Studies and the writing classes became writers' clubs as those involved just kept coming back for more. And who would have believed that classes entitled Jazz Ballet and Development and Dance would find groups quite willing to express themselves through dance in the morning!

We had an impressive cross section of learners who were of all ages, abilities and educational backgrounds, not that we even made enquiries into any of these. We maintained throughout an open approach, as *an tUachtarán* Mary Robinson was quick to observe when she used the word 'inclusive' to describe the programme. As part of that approach, we established links with special education groups and agencies. It was a delight to see the manner in which, for instance, learners from St Michael's House and Gheel were welcomed when they participated in classes and were encouraged and supported, not in any patronising way but rather accepted as members of the learning community.

All of these activities had to be housed and by the late nineties, classes were being held in four or five different locations. Furthermore, as funds became available and the adult education service began to expand significantly, I was unable to support the hard-pressed committee as I had done previously. But there was support from the hardworking and good-humoured administrative staff Celia Gaffney, Mary Ryan and Berni Fitzpatrick. Never daunted by hard work, the committee stuck with the task. Despite all of this growth and frantic activity and the increasing burden placed on the committee, it does not appear to have struck any chords in the places that mattered as the relentless pursuit of premises continued. From the start we had envisaged a building that would house a variety of adult education activities, including community education, the adult literacy scheme, education schemes for unemployed adults, a library, a crèche, a conference room and a canteen. We even imagined having a theatre as DATE had from the beginning engaged in the promotion of the arts, hosting at one stage a DATE Arts Week with a programme that included an art exhibition, a writers' evening, a drama evening and an *Oíche Cheoil.* Dream on!

Mary Cummins, Jo Pakenham and Billy McCluskey

## The Quest for Knowledge

It had been a wonderful adventure from the beginning as we set out on our journey, discovering and adapting as we went along. DATE, while not consciously presenting itself as a ground-breaking initiative, had in fact set down a blueprint and a way of proceeding that did offer a

Co. Dublin Vocational Education Committee
Dundrum Adult Training and Education

# D.A.T.E ARTS WEEK

Dundrum
23rd - 26th April 1991

## - PROGRAMME -

TUESDAY 23rd APRIL

10.00 a.m. - 12.30 p.m.
**D.A.T.E. Open Day** College of Commerce, Main Street, Dundrum.
(Adult Education Exhibition)

7.30 p.m.
**Reception and Official Opening** *(by invitation only)*
Robert Ballagh - Dundrum College, Sydenham Road.

**Art Exhibition** - D.A.T.E. Art Classes, Art & Design Class (Dundrum College)
**Local History Display**
On view throughout the week

---

WEDNESDAY 24th APRIL

8.00 p.m.
**Writers' Evening (Readings and Music)**
Ballinteer House, Dublin 16.
*(announcing the results of D.A.T.E. literary competitions)*

---

THURSDAY 25th APRIL

8.00 p.m.
**Drama Evening**
**Balally Players**
Special guest artist: *Brendan Cauldwell*
Marley Park Hotel. Admission £3.00

---

FRIDAY 26th APRIL

8.30 p.m.
**Oiche Cheoil**
Night of traditional music, song and dance.
Ballinteer House, Dublin 16.
*Cover charge: £1*

SEE OVER

DATE Arts Week

real challenge to existing paradigms of education and learning. First of all, there was the creation of an egalitarian democratic adult learning community where rigid hierarchical distinctions between principal and staff and between teachers and students were no longer accorded the same importance. The very simple practice of seating people in circles was in itself a clear statement that we had moved on from the old formalities where the teacher was the fount of all knowledge, wired for transmission only, and it emphasised that the learners were there on equal terms and that they too had a contribution to make. Here now was a forum where the valuable commodity on offer was knowledge, which was eagerly sought after and cherished. Many people who came found their lives enriched as they pursued opportunities they had previously been denied and brought to the table their own invaluable life experiences and stories. Those who have attended this centre over the years have variously described their experience as positive, fulfilling and even life-changing. Perhaps most important of all were the bonds of friendship and solidarity that were forged and strengthened over the years.

As part of the ongoing pursuit of a suitable premises, we had commenced negotiations with the relevant authorities at Dundrum Town Centre before I retired in 2004. My successor, Patricia Doran, continued these negotiations until finally they came to a successful conclusion in 2006 when DATE came to rest on the fifth floor in the new paradise of the Dundrum Town Shopping Centre, where I myself went and became a learner again.

****

# Recollection

**Dolores Byrne**, member and former chairperson of DATE.

I first came into contact with DATE shortly after it had been established. Some committee members were distributing brochures in the old Dundrum shopping centre. I joined a class which was held in the Old Taney school. Conditions were quite primitive but the class, taught by Maura Murphy, was really interesting. I went on to attend more classes and then was asked if I would like to help with the tea rota. Shortly after that, I was asked to join the committee. I must have passed some sort of test!

Since then, I have served as secretary once and chairperson twice. I can say with all honesty that DATE has given me more than I have ever given to DATE. I have found friendship and acceptance and the feeling that I am involved with something worthwhile has contributed to my self-esteem. I hope to keep going for another twenty years!

Mary Elliott and Dolores Byrne

# The Writing Phenomenon

From the very beginning, when the Writers' Group was first offered in the 1985 programme, it was clear that here was a course that would run and run. We were fortunate in that **Pauline Brady**, a gifted and sensitive teacher who already had experience leading writers' groups, was available. Writers I soon became Writers II, leading to the Writers' Workshop when well-known authors – novelists, journalists, dramatists and poets – were invited to come and help our learners.

In 1989, the group produced their first book, *The Fountain*, which was designed to showcase the talents of those participating in the group and which was then produced annually.

Here Pauline records her impressions of those early days.

## A Short Story

The story begins with the interview. A tall woman with a glorious smile and a child on her knee sits at a table in a crèche in the Old Taney School in Dundrum and invites me to work with a creative writing group. Her only advice is that the group should have fun. Between the interview and the first class, I prepare.

It is 1985. A statue moves miraculously in Ballinspittle and the Irish people show their amazing generosity through Live Aid. This event gives me the courage to walk through the door of DATE to meet its very first writers' group.

In the classroom I find generosity and what seems to me a kind of miracle. The group seated before me ticks all levels of writing experience and writing needs and it is the participants' great enthusiasm for the work of writing and their warmth towards the rookie tutor that comes as a surprise. So much so that an hour and a half later, I walk from the school, deleting from my mind all the group theory I had learned, or at least the forming, the norming and the storming parts. I decide, as wisely advised, to skip to the how-to-have-fun stage.

What follows seems like a ride on a rollercoaster. There is the fascinating fusion of imagination and language. There is the desire to find that elusive voice that distinguishes each writer. There is the hooking and the holding of the reader, that other human being, who, hopefully, will comprehend. Words like 'technique', 'theme', 'character', 'conflict' and 'plot' overflow from the classroom to the coffee counter where DATE committee members listen in and wonder how it will all end.

At this time the market for the unsolicited writing is good. By the second term, short stories, extracts from novels, poems, memoirs and articles are read into life in the classroom by their creators, then discussed, edited, re-read and finally submitted to publishers. Acceptance and rejection take on a whole new meaning and are either celebrated or dealt with as a matter of business. Among the group's fifteen writers, made up of thirteen women and two rather plucky men, there is much laughter and a lot of mischief. Friendships are forged and then, as in all good stories, somebody wants something they can't have and the words 'publish' and 'book' are spoken in the same sentence.

It's not as if we are the only characters in the story. There is the tall woman with the glorious smile and there are her colleagues, the other members of the DATE committee, who must feel they are now part of a fast-developing plot. Their support emboldens us to think about the 'book' but there are problems with time and a place in which the group can continue to meet.

This is where the man from the West enters the story, a kind of *deus ex machina* who sets convention aside and finds more weeks in an already spent term. From our start as a group of writers we now become proofreaders, editors, graphic designers, fundraisers and event planners. Even more time is found and, as if by magic, we become 'The Fountain Writers' Group' whose first collection of work, *The Fountain*, is launched on a balmy, climactic evening in June 1986.

In the years that follow, thanks to the inimitable man from the West and the ever-resourceful DATE committee, anything seems possible in Dundrum. The number of writers' groups grows. A Writers' Workshop is established and writers such as Eavan Boland, James Plunkett and John McGahern come to DATE's new address on Main Street to inspire and stimulate and to tell of even more ambitious

• *Dundrum Writers Group (left to right): Pauline Brady, Co-ordinator, Larry Murphy, Sile Doyle, Mary Webb, Pauline O'Reagan, Aine Miller, Muriel Bolger, Geraldine Whittaker, Brigid Kavanagh, Helen Sommers, and John O'Callaghan.    Missing from the picture are Lynn Pennefeather,. Anne O'Byrne, Ursula De Brun, Dolores Walshe and Gabrielle Clancy.*

DATE Writers' Group

horizons of achievement. *The Fountain* continues to be published. DATE writers find success as poets, playwrights, short story writers, memoirists and journalists. For some, special recognition comes in the form of literary awards and prizes.

The story goes on, though some of the characters change. New tutors bring fresh approaches, create their own narratives and the DATE writers continue to flourish. The DATE committee members, who have been at the core of the story, continue to do what they have always done in their quietly expert way. And the tall woman with the glorious smile? Her smile is still with us, particularly in the hearts of the characters in this story, those of us who were lucky enough to know her.

****

**George Ferguson** was a tutor with the Writers' Group for a number of years. A cheerful and kindly man, sadly he passed away in June 2014 but he is remembered with great affection by those who participated in his class. George not only offered advice and encouragement but every year led a group from his writing class to places of interest in Ireland and abroad. Shortly before he died, George, helpful as always, offered some constructive advice about this publication and how it might proceed. Here is an extract in which he reflects on his work with the Writers' Group.

# Creative Writing

I have long been convinced that writing is therapy. It provides an escape into the world of imagination and memory. When the writing is within a group, there is a bond of shared interest and mutual helpfulness. There is entertainment, encouragement and understanding. The bond becomes one of sympathy, caring and affection.

All of this I have found during my years with DATE and have been deeply moved by it. There is talent to be drawn out in everybody. Some express themselves well in poetry; some have unexpected humour; some master the short story and some with penetrating insight choose satire. There is indeed a novel in many but not everybody!

All students achieve publication in some form. It may be in reading to the weekly class. It may be in journals of local organisations as special interests. We have had publications ranging from fishing articles to bicycle marathons. Radio talks have been given by many. Biographies are always popular.

As a teacher, one of my proudest and most comforting memories is contained in the spontaneous comment of a faithful student who travelled to class from Wicklow. 'Tuesday morning is the highlight of the week.'

****

**Brigid Kavanagh** has been a part of the Writers' Group right from its very first meeting to the present day. Here is an extract from a piece that she wrote.

## DATE: Great Oaks from Little Acorns Grow

September 1985 and a group of strangers – thirteen women and two men – assembled in the Old Taney School in Dundrum to form the first writing class under the tutelage of Pauline Brady. I, for one, felt apprehensive as I was 'just a housewife' at home looking after my husband and family. Also, I knew none of the others as most came from the surrounding suburbs. I first had news of this new organisation from my daughter Mary, who was aware of my interest in writing and encouraged me to join.

And so it came to pass. The enthusiastic volunteers formed a committee and they were joined by other like-minded volunteers who have continued through the years to provide this wonderful service to the public.

In 1986, we produced the first copy of *The Fountain* without the aid of a computer, named after the fountain in Dundrum. The fountain had been erected in memory of Dr Isaac Usher who was killed in a horse and carriage accident.

In the early nineties, after Pauline Brady went on to other pursuits, our class was run by Aine Miller, one of the fifteen who had formed that first group. She has conducted two classes on Friday mornings ever since. In the intervening years, many of us have celebrated successes as articles from the group appeared in various publications.

Now we are enjoying the new premises in Dundrum where the accommodation on the fifth floor affords us an outstanding view of the Dublin mountains, sure to inspire us whenever the muse deserts us. Meanwhile, let the committee who made it possible take a bow.

****

When Pauline Brady decided to move to another branch of adult education, we wondered how she could be replaced but, in fact, we were fortunate to have a ready-made replacement. **Aine Miller** also began her writing career in Pauline's class and very quickly became an award-winning poet and prose writer. Here are Aine's thoughts on moving from the role of student to teacher.

## Just Imagine

Just imagine. Two words sum up the process that is the basis of the creative writing classes I run for DATE. What a privilege it is for me to face class after class, term after term, with those two words in my tool kit. 'Just imagine,' I say, then I wait to see what my students come up with. Housewives, nurses, doctors, dentists, accountants, teachers, even a private detective – enrolled for many different reasons – are given permission to release *la loca de la casa*, the madwoman of the house, the imagination. She is encouraged to roam freely, even promiscuously, with the other escapees from the humdrum worlds of shopping and school runs, business report writing and clock watching, the sudden unstructured ritual of retirement.

In the Friday morning classes we work to no particular schedule. It's not part of my brief to teach English grammar and punctuation or to correct any inadequacies in those fields. I aim for a happy, relaxed atmosphere and I have to say the happiest, most relaxed person is me and Friday is my favourite day of my week.

I encourage conversation. All kinds of subjects come up. The opinions aired float in the ether of the room to be picked up and reimagined at home in a quiet place, perhaps later transformed into a sparkling manuscript.

George Ferguson and Aine Miller

I don't think of myself as a teacher, more as a stimulator and initiator. I give clues, words, fishing lines. I provide pictures. We listen to poetry and I teach only the elements of form that are necessary to harness the wildness of imagination so that its produce is endlessly recoverable, endlessly re-experienceable. We produce a book of class writing each year. It used to be *The Fountain* magazine but now we have our own imprint, *The Bad Press*, Dundrum, usually available each autumn.

My contact with DATE goes back to their days in Eglinton Terrace when I, a mother of four schoolgoing children, enrolled in a craft class. I joined for company – adult company – above a shared activity. I found a welcoming and encouraging atmosphere. You enter a family when you join a DATE class. Friendship and sharing is the name of the game at DATE. It forms a parish of its own. I'm still in that parish now – I'm just at the other side of the desk. I admit to feeling sentimental about DATE and I experience an emotional overload when I recall the faces, the voices, the poems, stories, plays, jokes and riddles that have flooded my classrooms with colour over the years. They continue to colour my heart.

****

**Ursula de Brun**, another award-winning writer, was also a member of the first Writers' Group and she has succeeded George Ferguson as tutor at the DATE centre. She writes:

# DATE: A Space of Opportunity

I first encountered DATE on the day I slipped into Kilmacud church to have a time-out. I had been looking for a creative writing class for quite a while with no success and then pinned to the church door noticeboard was the heralding of a new class being run by an organisation in Dundrum.

Well, realising prayers could be answered, I hopped on my bike and scooted down to what I thought was the centre. I joined a rather long queue, mainly of young males, a queue that required a Garda presence. After ten minutes or so, I turned to one of the young males and asked, 'Are you here for the creative writing?' He looked at me like I'd lost my mind. 'What? Creative writing? This is the courts.'

The laughing Garda pointed me further along the road. I arrived red-faced and somewhat breathless to be told the class had just been filled. My disappointment was clear to the woman I was speaking to. 'Give me your number,' she said, 'and sure, if someone drops out, we'll give you a call.'

All the way up the long hill I was thinking: no one's going to drop out. And no one did. But I was back in the house when the phone rang and a voice said, 'What's one more? We'll fit you in.' This represents the sheer decency and kindness that was the forte of the wonderful set of women that made up the DATE committee. The person who had put up the notice in the church porch was later to become my dear friend, the late, great Ann McConnell.

Coming full circle, last year I joined the DATE project when I became tutor of the creative writing group. To see the familiar faces and get such a warm welcome was like coming home.

I know I am one of literally thousands who owe DATE a great debt of gratitude.

****

**Muriel Bolger** has forged a successful career as journalist, travel correspondent and novelist. Here she describes her busy life since 'graduating' from that first creative writing class.

# What a Difference a Class Made!

To say that time flies may seem like a cliché, but it is only when you look back you realise how quickly it really does speed by. You also realise what a difference certain events have made to your life.

Thirty years ago, I came back from a school run – the youngest had started secondary school and I was free. I made coffee and read a leaflet about DATE that would literally change my life. I read through it. I hadn't known there was such a thing as daytime adult education classes and I found many of the classes appealing, but it was the creative section that caught my eye. I rang the number. Enrolling day was over but someone had cancelled.

## Pauline Brady's Class

Later that week I found myself in Pauline Brady's class in an old school room beside the former courthouse in Dundrum. The aspiring scribes included John O'Callaghan, Larry Murphy, Ursula de Brun, Aine Miller, Ann McConnell, Lynn Pennefather, Dolores Walsh, Sile Doyle, Brigid Kavanagh, Mary Woods and Mary Webb. Several have since gone from us but I am feel enriched to have known them and to have shared happy times together.

The classes were described as educational and that may well have been the case, but what I got from them was so much more. I got laughter and friendship, great conversations and the enjoyment of common interests, not to mention tea and coffee addictions from volunteering to do the coffees on Tuesdays with Ann McConnell. We had moved to bigger classrooms in the College of Commerce on the Main Street by then.

Bit by bit people got published, usually in Sean McCann's feature pages in the *Evening Press* and by the late Noeleen Dowling in her Pettitcoat Panel on Thursdays. The excitement was fantastic. Some had radio pieces on *Sunday Miscellany* and *Just a Thought* and each success only fed our enthusiasm. Then Dolores Walsh had a book published – *Where the Trees Weep*. Such classmates couldn't but inspire and make you want to write more than the short pieces we did every week.

However, life and family commitments got in the way of the classes but not in the way of writing for many of us who started out in DATE. We rejoiced in the successes over the years as Aine Miller was announced the Patrick Kavanagh Poet for her collection *Goldfish in a Baby Bath*. She has featured in many collections since. Ursula de Brun's plays have been staged in Dublin and around the country. She was the P.J. O'Connor and Francis McManus prize winner on RTÉ while Lynn Pennefather won the Power's short story competitions and the list goes on and on.

## A New Departure

My own writing journey began that first morning in DATE and led directly to being allowed to sit in the newsroom in *The Irish Press* for work experience at the ripe old age of forty-one. In Burgh Quay, I stepped into a whole new world of enormous typewriters that went clickety-clack, the smell of printer ink and the manic but intoxicating frenzy of a newsroom. I also met a kaleidoscope of characters – chancers (like me), alcoholics, brilliant writers, wits and raconteurs.

I was sent on my first travel press trip and that was when my double life began – one side of which involved five-star luxury and Michelin dining, camel and helicopter rides, secluded beaches and glitzy cruises and a career as a travel writer; the other saw me juggling mortgage repayments and raising three opinionated teenagers.

In the features department, my brief was to interview incoming authors on their book tours. Consequently I spent many wonderful hours drinking tea in the Shelbourne, the Merrion and the Westbury hotels, chatting with the likes of Douglas Kennedy, Mary Wesley, Nelson de Mille, Sue Townsend, Ken Follet, Polly Devlin and Jilly Cooper. Others like Frank Delaney, Barbara Taylor Bradford, Jeffrey Archer and Robert Ludlum merited lunches – long memorable lunches. I was in my element meeting these people.

Journalism kept me busy. It took me into the world of interiors, visiting design shows in Madrid, Lisbon, Frankfurt and Copenhagen, a glass-blowing contest in Finland, garden shows at Chelsea and Tatton Park and flea markets in Paris and Amsterdam. I spent days on photographic shoots at ostentatious, tasteful and quirky houses and in wonderful gardens around the country. In short, I revelled in what I was doing.

I cruised the Mediterranean, the Caribbean, the North Sea, through the Panama Canal and wrote about the different destinations I visited. In between, I penned brochures for mattresses, home insulation, cities of Ireland, garden centres and property companies. I even wrote a magazine for truckers!

Then I was asked to write a sort of guidebook – *Darting About* – capturing snippets about the famous people associated with the various DART stops from Howth to Greystones. It was fittingly launched at Pearse Station.

## Becoming a Novelist

Becoming a novelist was never my intention. It was almost accidental. I wrote a rare short story on the beach in Cyprus and the more I thought about it the more I felt I could possibly expand it. I only ever worked on it when I was travelling (laptops had become the norm by then). It grew slowly and my New Year's resolution for 2010 was to try and get published, so I sent it off. It was called *Consequences*.

Coincidentally that was the year Dublin was given the UNESCO City of Literature title. I hadn't heard of anyone bringing out a book about all the writers associated with my native city, so I approached a publisher with the idea. The late and ever-gracious Mary Webb, from our original DATE class, was by now a director with O'Brien Press. As luck would have it, I was asked to present myself in the morning at Hachette Ireland regarding the novel and at the O'Brien Press regarding the non-fiction work in the afternoon on the same day. By lunchtime, I was sipping champagne in a friend's house, celebrating a two-book fiction deal. Later the celebrations included a third as the literary idea had been commissioned too. That one even got a ministerial book launch in Dublin Castle with Lee Dunne as the guest speaker.

As I sit here working on novel number five, is it any wonder that I often find myself pondering the enormous difference that first creative writing class made to my life? It changed it dramatically. It paid my bills and filled my life with interesting people and places, new achievements and, most precious of all, wonderful friends with whom I've been able to share it.

Olivia Mitchell TD, Muriel Bolger, Olive Carroll

****

# Recollection

**Maureen Flynn**, a long-serving member of the DATE committee, recalls her experience of creative writing at DATE.

When I joined in 1987, DATE had up and running for three years. I joined the Creative Writing class. You could feel the buzz and excitement going in every Tuesday, as students gathered round the tea table in the prefab, having tea and coffee and chatting to others who were coming out from earlier classes.

The Creative Writing class was run by Pauline Brady, who guided us through the problems of getting our thoughts down on paper, whether fact or fiction. There was a great feeling of fun and camaraderie in the class and some of the people I met at that writing class have remained friends to this day.

With Maura in the English class we read Shakespeare, Scott Fitzgerald, Thomas Hardy and many more. One student was asked on returning from her holidays how she had enjoyed herself. 'Everything was grand,' she replied, 'but my husband complained that I was spending too much time with Michael Henchard.' We were reading *The Mayor of Casterbridge* at the time.

Helping with the teas at that time, I was told by a friend that I had landed myself a 'nice cushy little job', not realising that we were all volunteers and indeed still are. Being on the committee, as well as being tea-makers, we all became what the Australians call 'removalists'. Having only three classrooms in the prefabs, we seemed to be always moving tables and chairs from one place to another, especially for enrolling days. We were younger then and bad backs didn't worry us.

Later, we also had classes in the Dom Marmion Centre, in rooms under the Holy Cross church and in the Holy Cross school. The rooms under the church were damp and sometimes cold and the steps that led down to them could be difficult for some but, to the credit of both teachers and students, everyone in the classes held there survived.

The late George Ferguson brought his writers' class on many interesting trips, including a most enjoyable cruise to Norway. We had gardening outings, visits to galleries here, in Paris, London and Amsterdam.

From the time when the original committee sat down in a pub in Dundrum to organise a few classes to the present day when we have almost seventy classes and over 1,000 students, DATE has certainly come a long way.

But one thing hasn't changed. Go into the tea room any day and listen to the discussions and banter among the students, sometimes in Irish, sometimes in French or Spanish or German, and you will find the same enthusiasm and enjoyment that has remained right through the thirty years of DATE classes.

*Ta súil agam to mbeidh DATE anseo i nDún Droma ar feadh i bhfad.*

# 'Second-Chance Education'

'Second-chance education' was the expression in vogue back then and it referred to those wishing to return to learning after an absence. But it had a special resonance for those who had missed out on second- and third- level education the first time round and who now wanted to put that right. At DATE, we made every effort to accommodate those who were returning, whether simply to prove to themselves that they were capable of achieving Intermediate and Leaving Cert. standards or who had more ambitious goals in mind.

Here are the thoughts of **Roisin O'Donnell**, who guided many students to 'exam' success in the early days and who later presented very enjoyable and very well-attended courses in history and politics.

## The First Thirty Years

There was something stirring beneath the surface of gloom in the 1980s. It wasn't a plot to subvert the system (although that would have been perfectly understandable in this decade of broken promises and frequent elections); it was more a movement of self-help. Groups were forming to put together ideas that might lift them out of the doldrums.

One such group found itself in the hall under Dundrum church in April of 1984 and before the meeting ended, a committee was give the task of founding an adult education centre for the area.


## The Vagaries of Chance

It was one of those occasions when the vagaries of chance do a better job than careful selection because this group of individuals together sparked a rare dynamism. Theories swirled about in those early days. The new centre, they all agreed, would have none of the fears and sweats of schooldays of old. It was going to be a return-to-learning incubator rather than a school, a place where horizons would be broadened, minds lifted, where students would gain a weightless addition to their mental repertoire. Above all, no one was to leave feeling a lesser person than before.

Much effort was put into giving students a sense of place. But place was the very thing that was absent in those days. So begging and borrowing (stopping short of stealing) resulted in classrooms being made available in the local area.

DATE might have got off the ground with a whole lot less verve were it not for the AEO, Liam Bane, who infused everything with his easy-going style while he worked with rabid determination. If these two seem contradictory, it is because they were and it was this collision, like a meteoric bang, that made the result so powerful. Few students knew Liam had a surname, much less a scholarly title, because he wore his learning lightly.

Into this humming atmosphere returning students came in their droves. My first group sat Leaving Cert. History in June 1988. The small but select set who persevered to the end said the shared joy of seeing it through was worth every step of the struggle along the way. Later, when I met those who had not persisted, they said how much they regretted not having seen it through, that in retrospect the paper was far easier than it looked through the worried eyes of a looming exam. No one ever expressed regret for having finished the course and so when students began to have second thoughts as June approached I told them this to stop them taking fright in mid-stream.

Students became fully immersed in their studies. At times it seemed as if all other aspects of the world had been eclipsed. They fell for celebrated figures. They found Parnell's standoffishness ever so alluring. The handsome Davitt lost one arm as a result of the cruel Darwinian conditions of capitalism, which made him all the more romantic. They cheered on Collins as he cycled openly up O'Connell Street despite the generous bounty on his head. A less understandable favourite was Rasputin, who 'definitely had something' for one woman. My colleague, Maura Murphy, reported despairingly from her English class that someone had taken a fancy for Iago, the villain who betrayed Othello. Male students were not so taken with female historical figures and perhaps that is because there were so few to choose from.

Past students reported that, nice and all as passing exams was, it was nothing compared to the spin-off effects. They could understand the news a whole lot better. They had gained enough self-assurance to throw an opinion or two into a conversation or take on the puffed-up know-alls whose views they would not have questioned once upon a time. That alone was a worthwhile achievement.

Leisure classes had none of the tensions of exams. No deadlines made for easy-going exchanges of views though discussion flowed out of hand at times, prompting neighbouring classes to complain about the noise, especially the Politics class. Leinster House was never so obstreperous and, unlike the Dáil, we did not have the power of ejection.

## Enrolling Times

DATE was at its most buoyant at enrolling times. Classrooms pulsed with long queues, lists of names, quick-stepped committee members, hard-pressed money counters. It was first come, first served effervescence. Examination classes found it hardest to earn their keep and we used to cast wistful side glances at our relaxed colleagues who folded up their enrolling sheets smugly at the end of the first day – full, *complet, lán go doras* – while for us, the nail-biting task had only begun. How to fill a class of the required eight minimum for English, History, Classical Studies, A-level Politics … So we dug deep for inspiration on how to encourage students to make the exam commitment.

Exam popularity thrived in hard times and it finally flowed to its death not from failure but from too much success. One heady morning we woke up to find every square inch of suburbia turned to gold without a single sod being turned. As the economy ripped into full steam, toil-less wealth triumphed over the slow incremental process of learning. An exam result – lovely and all as it looked on a framed certificate – was no match for wall-to-wall ostentation, four-wheeled driving and multi-property-owning, Armani-wearing excess.

Politicians went abroad to teach others how they too could be as prosperous as Ireland. The lesson was simple – play off tomorrow against today (a lesson we never taught in DATE). Alas, tomorrow came and one day pinstriped troika men arrived to tell us a thing or two about ourselves, wielding, for emphasis, the knives of reform.

DATE has seen the transition through like a wise old lady (excuse the sexism), unshaken by the ups and downs of economic success and failure. The crowds still enliven the shopping centre on enrolling day. The steady work of continuity is safe in the hands of Patricia Doran and the many members of that same committee who have stuck with adult education for three decades now.

****

**Maura Murphy** is perhaps the longest-serving teacher in DATE. She was there on that very first morning, offering advice and encouragement, as always, and has just retired this year. Maura will be remembered for her selfless dedication and her total commitment and determination to ensuring that her students would be successful the second time around.

# A Second Chance

I didn't really know what it meant to learn until I started teaching. Through teaching I learned how to learn and I hope I succeeded in helping others in their unique quest for knowledge.

My odyssey began when I was offered an English Leaving Cert. class at a new adult education centre in Dundrum. I was both excited and apprehensive. I was excited at the prospect of teaching adults literature, of exploring the great dramatic characters of Shakespearean tragedy, entering the enthralling world of the Victorian novelists, encountering the mysterious and enchanted Romantic poets. But I was also a little apprehensive about facing the unknown. There was no template for us to follow. As teacher and students we were ploughing a new furrow, venturing into uncharted territory.

And yet there was a sense of freedom about those early days. The class was outside the strict system of institutional education, a friendly voluntary group ran the centre, everybody was on first-name terms. Even the classroom had been a library in its previous life. The whole atmosphere was informal and easy-going and everyone was ready to forge ahead with a unity of purpose.

## The First Year

My first meeting with the class was filled with a sense of anticipation and expectancy. It was held in the library, a small room with big east-facing windows. It always seemed to be sunny, although maybe I was so caught up in the new class, I just didn't notice the darker, rainy days. The students also seemed to radiate eagerness and energy for the task that lay ahead. Reality strikes! I ran home to study and haven't stopped studying since!

That first year we were carried along on a wave of enthusiasm. I suppose we were rescued from panic by the innocence of being beginners, unaware of the traps and snares we might happen across.

From the success of that first Leaving Cert. class, we boldly took on the higher level. Later, the exam programme further expanded to include Group, Inter and Junior Cert. and this programme was given the title 'Second-Chance Education'. It was indeed a second chance for us all to try another mode of learning. It is rare that we get a second chance in life, another try at something that didn't work the first time around, whether in our relationships, our studies or our work. What wouldn't we give for another attempt, another shot, another throw of the dice? But here it was, that gift-opportunity, not only to confront the regrets and perceived failure of our past experiences but also to realise what was secretly hoped for.

However, the task was huge. There were many challenges, both for the students and the teacher. For some, their early experience of school had promoted states of fear, constant anxiety sapping their youthful energy and preventing them from applying themselves to learning. This could result in a sense of failure and disappointment, leaving a residue of debilitating self-doubt. So the very act of coming to an exam class was not only daunting but courageous. Furthermore, as adults they had to set aside time, some from work, others from rearing a family and running a home. All of that involved terrific effort and risk. But their willingness to learn and engage with various texts stayed strong despite the obstacles. They very often arrived at the exam class after many earlier attempts in their search. The lengths that some were prepared to go to to reach their goal filled me with admiration and respect, even more so as I read accounts of their earlier school experiences. I can only consider it a privilege to have had the opportunity to encourage them to achieve their own particular dream.

For myself as a teacher, there were also challenges. The greatest was the time constraint, fitting a two-year course into seven months. We had to bring students from a variety of backgrounds, abilities and readiness levels and try to achieve a standard so they could take the exam with some expectation of success. We also had to tackle a different approach to learning, especially in the poetry section. Gone were the days of just learning chunks of poems off by heart. Now the students were encouraged to participate in their own learning and come to an understanding of the poem in terms of its theme, image, sound and how these are interwoven to shape the poem's meaning. The groundwork was done through questions that sent the reader back again and again to the poem. So with patience and sometimes despair, we moved slowly, preparing the ground.

Slowly trust was built up between student and teacher as we laboured together through the tough, ground-breaking work with its 'sheer plod'. It required discipline to stay with it, especially the poetry and the study of Shakespeare. Then came the time to cut and run! You think when you have conquered one poem or one page of Shakespeare that you are set up only to find yourself back at zero again. But actually you are building up knowledge. You just have to persevere, regardless of the frustration.

## The Exam

The mock exam was a turning point in the year and the students found it an invaluable exercise. From this trial run they learned what was required for the real exam. As well as that, they discovered that the exam wasn't a vast insurmountable unknown – in fact, it was quite specific and, most important of all, success was achievable! This insight gave them the courage to clear up any niggling anxieties. Now there was no hesitation in asking questions or even fear of making mistakes. The gloves were off!

This was my favourite time of year – spring coming into summer when 'the May month flaps its glad green leaves like wings' (T. Hardy). It was a time when the relationship between student and teacher came into its own, as if both had been tested and found acceptance. Certainly we were all together in this. It was very satisfying to see this transformation, to see students lose themselves in the text. Now they showed a new confidence in expressing their own opinions, a new self-belief. This for me was as good, if not better, than any 'A' result in the exam.

After the exam we all gathered in the pub. There was such excitement as students arrived from various centres (this was in the early days before we had our own exam centre). It was like welcoming home runners from a marathon event, each of whom had a story to tell. For everyone, it was a great relief – it was over, finished, completed. They had done it. Results didn't seem to matter – that was for another day.

That other day arrived and brought with it its own satisfaction and rewards. And so the years passed and each September we began the journey anew – new hopes, new dreams, new beginnings. And along the way, I was somehow led back to where it all began, to ancient Greece and Rome. This seemed a natural progression as our study of English literature is steeped in echoes and voices from the classical world. Little did I realise the harvest this would yield. We were all astonished by the depth and breadth of their own vision and, at the same time, amazed by the familiar echoes that resonate through time right down to the present – from Homer's epics to Greek tragedy and Greek philosophers like Socrates, Plato and Aristotle who confronted the burning questions of their day with a 'free and fearless enquiry'. That they are still relevant in our modern, technological world is highlighted in a *Newsweek* interview in 2001 with Steve Jobs who said 'I would trade all of my technology for an afternoon with Socrates'.

The nature of the subject was reflected in the spirit of the class in its variety and diversity. All had a keen curiosity about the subject and students generously shared their ideas from their own unique viewpoints, thus keeping our explorations and discussions lively and democratic. The tempo when we strayed off the beaten track to explore and discover was intense at times but mostly light-hearted and leisurely. It seemed once the Greek and Roman spark was ignited, it would light our way indefinitely. It was a wondrous and inspirational odyssey.

All this was made possible by a unique mix of elements that came together to create a centre of learning. The voluntary committee ensured a vibrant yet safe environment with their humour, flexibility and humanity. From the very beginning, the students came first and this ethos held fast. The second element in the mix was Liam Bane, the official person in charge of the operation and the link to state funding. He was more of a colleague than a boss. There was a mutual respect and trust between us. More than that, he was encouraging, accessible and good-humoured, against all the odds! His tour at the beginning of the year was a drop-in visit where he stood at the door, welcomed everyone and told us to enjoy it! I must say too that I have also found Liam's successor, Patricia Doran, to be most supportive and kind. The teachers, those wandering minstrels, loved their subjects and seemed only delighted to sing to anyone who would listen – especially like-minded souls.

The coming together of these elements created an energy and a space that brought out the best in everyone and everyone just wanted to give their best to make it work. It really was a second chance for all of us. Of course it is only in retrospect that this dynamic can be described. Back then, we were all too intent on living it.

Leaving Cert. English, 1985

Maura Murphy and Eileen Deegan (student) in earnest discussion

# Student Responses

And here are the views and memories of some students who participated in those classes.

**Christine McMahon** writes:

I was in the middle of one of those spring-cleans – you know the kind where you spend more time looking at old photographs and wondering just how much rubbish can one person accumulate in a lifetime – when I came across an old handwritten receipt. Why was the date so familiar? 23 September 1991. It wasn't a birthday, an anniversary or, God forbid, a death. So why did it resonate so much? And then it dawned on me. It was the receipt from the day I first enrolled with DATE. A day, I can safely say, that changed my life forever.

As with a lot of momentous events in life, it didn't announce itself with a fanfare of bells and whistles. Rather it unfolded with all the familiar mundanity of a working day. But beneath the apparent normality coursed a seaside bucket and spade excitement! A sense of anticipation laced with low-level dread mounted as the morning progressed. The die was cast. The cap was over the orchard wall and I had no choice but to follow it. Park the bike, up the gangplank, in the door.

A delirium of activity, a rush of noise, a kaleidoscope of images. Was I the only one in the place who didn't know where to go or what to do? Hold your nerve. It had taken years to get this far. Not the right time, too busy, too expensive. No energy, no confidence, no space. And yet, miraculously, here was the time and this was the space. And what an inauspicious space it appeared to be at first glance. From the modest, almost apologetic exterior of the prefab, tucked away from the main street, stoic as an unassuming relative, to the utilitarian, faded interior, the magnitude of its intent was in no way evident. I jumped into the fray. The room crowded, tables erected with makeshift signs ('History!' 'English!' 'French!'), a sea of noise. Deep breath and join the queue. And then suddenly it was alright. 'You will love Maura,' says the lady as I enrol and she hands me my receipt. These people who only a few minutes earlier I had thought of as all-seeing and all-knowing were in fact volunteers, fellow pilgrims on the road to learning. They too had embarked on this journey and were living proof of not just survival but also evolution and belonging. This was my first experience of DATE. And it was indicative of the warm and inclusive atmosphere of the safe space where our fledgling hopes were nurtured.

And so began our journey. From disparate, at times desperate, individuals to a focused harmonious unit. With bent heads and open hearts we excavate the glorious patchwork landscape of English literature. In my mind's eye I see us, intent and concentrated, with the rapt attention of children. And in that time and place we dwelt in a state of grace, 'we few, we happy few'. It wasn't familial bonds that bound us, but something almost as sacred. It was a reflected sensibility. It was a yearning, a hunger, a loss, a belief that man does not live by bread alone, that we are more than the sum of the parts. Here in this safe harbour we were granted immunity from the demands of work and family. Here, indeed, we were 'free in the oriental streets of thought'.

## First Faltering Steps

Here we took our first faltering steps, guided and nourished at every turn. I remember as a child my mother used to light the fire and if it didn't take she would put a sheet of newspaper up to cover it, to let it 'draw'. I was fascinated by how the flame would ignite and whoosh up the chimney amid wild consternation. What drama, what magic! But I was secure in the knowledge that we were safe, we were home and no harm could befall us there. The class contained that element of sanctuary coupled with a sense of joyous anticipation. It strengthened our backs, deepened our understanding and honed our skills. Something only glimpsed, only hinted at, was given flesh and bone. Bonds were forged in the white heat of battle (exams), but we were not conscripts. Friendships are anchored in a mutual vision, with a shared journey and hoped-for destination. It instils in us a self-belief, facilitates and helps us navigate the uncharted waters of state exams. Above all it is an exploration. At times the boat may be leaky, the weather grey, the horizon a distant, seemingly unattainable goal. But a reciprocal striving, a delight in discovery and a joy in each other's achievements prevail. There is a democracy of learning, an elation and a despair, probably in equal measure. But with the aid of our connection with each other, we bear witness to an inner life and to a shared humanity.

The exam is a concrete validation of our strivings. It is a transformative rite of passage. It changes not only how we view ourselves but also how the world views us. And it transforms how we see the world. The exam is a valid currency. Our passport has been stamped. The world has opened up to us, survivors of a flawed, often brutal and brutalising, Irish educational system, of the casual cruelty inflicted that stunted, stalled and at times broke the green sap of young hearts and minds. Here we were healed; we were made whole, re-imagined. For what is adult education but re-birth, a chance to re-imagine yourself – to re-instigate and re-envisage the world?

It is said that character manifests itself in great moments, but is made in small ones. Not the events as such – they are the punctuation; the full stops and capital letters, the exclamation marks. The process is the narrative, a process facilitated and nurtured on all levels. From Liam (blessed amongst women!), the bulwark at our back, to the unseen, unsung committee members who worked ceaselessly in the background. As well as the office staff who welcomed us and put us at ease, Eilish and the girls in the crèche who made it possible, the volunteers who made tea, baked cakes, raised funds and generally imbued DATE with the warmth and welcome of a home-away-from-home. We must also acknowledge Maura (and later Roisin), who kindled our flickering (and at times dying) self-belief and demonstrated the transformative and restorative power of learning. Both Maura and Roisin are living proof of Henry Adam's assertion that 'a teacher affects eternity'. Their belief and vision got us drunk on the heady air of shimmering possibilities.

No man is an island and DATE is a shining example of this. It epitomised community – grassroots, organic, non-hierarchical, people power. It is a living testament to the power for good that like-minded, dedicated, visionary people can harness. 'Dundrum' is now a byword for commercialism, a Mecca of materialism, part of our brash, brave new world, but in our hearts Dundrum will always chime to a different, distant, gentler beat, to a time of beginnings, awakenings, realisations. It gave us back our voice. And as Seamus Heaney said, 'If you have the words, there's always a chance that you'll find the way'.

And **Patricia Court** writes:

I have no happy memories of my schooldays as a child and I left school at an early age, so why was I, nearly twenty years later, enrolling for an 'Enjoying English' class in DATE? Deep within myself I knew there had to be more to education than fear and lack of confidence.

After my first day in Maura Murphy's class, I knew I was right. For me, she was an inspiring and dedicated teacher. She opened my eyes to the wonderful world of literature. I recall some lively discussions on Jane Austen, Shakespeare, the Brontës and so on. Compared to my younger days, this was a wonderful experience and I wanted it to continue, so I decided to study for the Inter Cert.

A couple of years later I sat the exam. This brought many challenges as the preparation for it was very difficult. I was juggling family life, home and caring for an aged parent. However, when I received my results, I knew it had all been worthwhile. I was very happy to have completed the course and the sense of achievement was enormous.

Liam Bane and the dedicated DATE volunteers were always helpful and supportive. A huge bonus for me was the lasting friendships I made. It was wonderful to share a variety of experiences with other students. Indeed, many years later we still meet each other!

My confidence in my own abilities has been restored. The classrooms we now share have come a long way from the fearful ones where I spent my young life. I believe this is thanks to the adult education system that we can still enjoy today.

I wish DATE continued success.

The reflections of **Maire Redmond**:
Leaving school at a very early age leaves one with very little confidence. The classroom in the 1940s and '50s was a daunting place. Fear was part of every day! As a child, seeing a teacher's cane dangling from her desk was a constant reminder of the consequences of not keeping quiet. It was a frightening experience not to know the correct answer to a question. How could a child learn in those circumstances? As an adult it never occurred to me that returning to adult education would help me regain confidence in my learning abilities until I met someone who was just like me. She told me of her experience of going back as an adult to re-educate herself. She joined DATE and never regretted it. So with her encouragement I made my way back.

Starting back was an unnerving experience to say the least. The memories of the past came flooding back as I sat at a desk in the classroom for the first time in over thirty years. I remember thinking, 'If people don't turn up and the class is cancelled, sure at least I've tried.' Such negativity was part and parcel of who I was at that time. In my first class I was fortunate to be taught by a very dedicated English teacher called Maura Murphy. In a privileged class of six, I learned quite a lot that would have escaped me in my younger days in a class of fifty-two. It was an exam class and I had to work very hard to achieve my goal. However, it was a great experience and I was very happy with my result. I met some lovely people and to this day we are still on one another's Christmas card lists.

I went on to study Leaving Cert. English. Again I had the privilege of being taught by two very dedicated teachers, Pauline Brady and Carole Dunbar. My knowledge of poetry in my younger days was limited to rhyming it parrot-fashion but in that class I learned about the poet and the meaning that poetry is meant to convey. It was really hard work as I was in the normal situation of having to care for my family and be there for them. I did complete the course and was once again very happy with the outcome.

Over the next few years I enjoyed many courses at DATE. I also became a tutor with the Adult Literacy Scheme run by Carole Dunbar.

This was a very worthwhile experience because I could identify closely with the needs of others.

My last experience of adult education was in the College of Commerce, Dundrum, where I enrolled for two years in Office Technology, a course funded by the European Union. There were eight modules to be studied to qualify for a diploma. It was a brilliant course and we all benefitted from it. And again, I made many friends with common interests.

Shortly after completing this course, I was offered a part-time position as secretary to the Adult Literacy Scheme and I was very happy there until my retirement.

A date . . . with the fruits of two years' hard work

● *Valerie Coombes, art teacher, at the Dundrum Adult Training and Education Open Day in Dundrum, Co. Dublin, yesterday.*

The first Open Day – Valerie Coombes, art tutor

Mary Cummins and Mary Elliott

Kay Bailey, Olive Carroll, John O'Callaghan, Mary Cummins

I gained so much in all those years and one thing that stands out for me is the respect that I received from teachers. When I began my journey, I was an adult with little confidence being supported by teachers who understood and did everything to help me. This enabled me to gain confidence in my own abilities and I am extremely grateful to all of these people.

A visit to the Áras with President Mary McAleese

Backs to the wall – the DATE committee with Kathleen Berigan and Tom Newman

Celebrating Mary Elliott's appointment as Cathaoirleach of Dun Laoghaire
Rathdown Co. Council

DATE committee, 1994

**Sheelagh Nugent** describes the journey that led her to further education:

# From Leaving Cert. English Student to College Graduate

When I joined DATE back in the late 1980s, I was a stay-at-home wife and mother with little education. Attending class was a means to escape the house for a couple of hours and a way of doing something different to routine housework. I went along for social reasons, but I was open to learning new skills. As a child I had experienced a lot of illness, which resulted in long years of hospitalisation. As a result, my formal education was fairly limited but my basic literacy skills were fine – or so I thought. They may have needed a little tweaking.

So it was with a false air of confidence that I sat down in Pauline Brady's Creative Writing class. I was not used to being in a classroom set-up so I recall how my heart pounded and my stomach churned that first day. I remember how my voice stuck in my throat till only a low squeak came forth when I was called upon to speak.

As part of the class we would write short stories and articles that we had to read aloud and, worse still, we then had to listen to feedback from the class. When the feedback was favourable, I revelled in it but when it proved unfavourable, I had to grit my teeth and learn to accept the constructive criticism. I gained enormous confidence in Pauline's class as she made me believe that I could write well. I was so encouraged by her comments that I continue to scribble but I am still awaiting that bestseller.

I came to feel safe at DATE and participated in all sorts of leisure classes until eventually I took the plunge and decided to do some state exams. English at Leaving Cert. level presented an enormous challenge but my naivety knew no bounds. I told the excellent English teacher

Maura Murphy that I would sit the exam at honours level despite having no experience of exams at any level. I was stressed because of the exam, had nightmares, woke up covered in beads of sweat and believed that I would be Maura's first failure. I studied the books morning, noon and night till my head was addled.

The day of the exam dawned and I felt sick but somehow I made it to the school hall. I remember being handed the paper and feeling like death. I stared at the paper, seeing the print dance until it resembled Sanskrit. Taking a deep breath, I calmed down, read the paper, scribbled answers and prayed they made sense. Needless to say, my exam technique was not up to scratch but I ploughed on. To my astonishment I got a decent honour.

My next foray was Leaving Cert. history. Again I was plagued by doubts and those recurring nightmares ensued but thanks to Roisin O'Donnell's excellent tutoring, I managed to obtain an honour on the honours paper.

Bitten by the bug, I found I had an insatiable thirst for knowledge. I took an extramural certificate course with Maynooth University, which was facilitated by John Drennan, now a political journalist. I was on a roll. I took a pre-university course but did not believe that I could ever attend such a prestigious institution. I had no role models to guide me and I felt too old to tread this difficult path. Leave it to the youngsters, I thought.

## Time to Move On

I hung on at DATE like a schoolgirl reluctant to leave secondary school. I had made lots of friends and the teachers were accessible and friendly. I was comfortable in the safe space of DATE and I had all but exhausted the courses on offer. It was time to move on. I needed to prove to myself that I could go out and engage with the big world. And so it was that little old me sent in my CAO application form. Perhaps they won't accept me, I thought, but wonder of wonders, they did. I was in turmoil. What could I expect from an institution like

UCD? It would surely be an anonymous place where I would never fit in. I remember trying to slide into the wall when I took my seat at my first lecture. The workload was huge, the study rewarding, reading list humongous. However, I must say it was a great place to be. Being older, I felt I would not connect with the younger students but I found them to be polite, great fun and very helpful – and I had the craic too. I'd like to say the exams were a doddle but no, the stress left me exhausted. I felt privileged to be in university and never forgot that it was DATE that got me there. I completed an arts degree (BA Hons), a higher diploma and subsequently a master's degree. I still harbour notions of completing a PhD.

When I cast my mind back to that September of long ago, I realise that my life's journey took a new and welcome turn when I enrolled at DATE. It was there that I gained my basic education. It was the people there who nurtured me and instilled in me a love of lifelong learning. My sincere thanks to all those wonderful people involved: to the DATE committee members who I know do Trojan work; to Liam Bane who oversaw proceedings with good-humoured expertise; to the dedicated teachers who gave so much of themselves; to the many who created a pleasant learning environment – long may they continue their good work! Finally thank you to my fellow students and friends at DATE who provided me with friendship and rewarding company throughout the years.

# Further Education Courses

Over a number of years, in collaboration with NUI Maynooth and UCD, courses were offered that afforded students the opportunity to obtain certificates with a view of advancing to third-level education or seeking employment. The counselling course was hugely popular and always attracted large numbers. **Terry Tynan**, who participated in several DATE classes, describes her experiences as a student in the counselling programme and her subsequent career.

## Wheels within Wheels

While still in its infancy, I joined DATE to study counselling in 1984/85 as a potential career move. The atmosphere was accepting, caring, welcoming to all. The idea of counselling, being pretty new to Irish society at that time, meant that a number of renowned therapists from other countries came to DATE willingly so that we novices could benefit from their experience. In 1986, two of us attended the World Conference of Counsellors at Carysfort College where we met our counterparts from around the world, including downtown Chicago gangland therapists and counsellors from New York and Singapore.

Roaming the grounds at break times was a colourful and enriching experience. It was also quite daunting to realise that I, a newly initiated counsellor, might be called on to do what these people were doing. And all thanks to the imminent availability of education for adults in my neighbourhood.

I have always derived a great sense of excitement when exposed to new ideas, fresh thinking and the opening up of new worlds. After a break from study for about ten to fifteen years (my education during that period was of a different kind entirely as I gave birth to and raised four sons), I enjoyed the continuity of study in DATE, one subject leading to the next. A small group of us who took the Maynooth Diploma in Counselling set up a counselling practice and continued to study. Our services were made available when we were requested to work out of a local community centre. We worked there for a couple of years with modest success until each one of us developed a speciality that appealed to us – art, teaching parenting, grief therapy. This was quite a remarkable group of women and all of us had come from DATE.

A number of years later, I went back to university and took a first class honours BA and a master's degree. I have no doubt that DATE not only helped to improve my confidence but also laid the foundation stone for these achievements.

All of it has been part of the rich journey of self discovery. May the universe always shower abundance on the wonderful generous souls who have helped to paint the way in vivid colour in the Dundrum Adult Education Centre.

****

Another course, Liberal Studies, was run in conjunction with NUI Maynooth, was the choice of many students and, for a time, this course was presented by **John Drennan**, who later went on to forge a career in journalism. He is now a respected commentator on political affairs and is the Political Editor with the *Sunday Independent*. Here are John's memories of those times.

# Tea, Biscuits and a Place Where I Often Learned More than the Students

Convention suggests that if you are a teacher, the students you have should learn more than you, the educator.

However, during my time at the DATE series of morning classes, it was often difficult to discern who was doing the teaching and who was doing the learning.

For a period I presented a somewhat grandiosely titled 'Liberal Studies' course, which was centred on culture, politics and ideology in Ireland at the turn of the nineteenth century. It was set at the intellectually challenging level of a third-level degree course. When I arrived to teach my first class and saw a group of pleasant ladies smiling up at me, I wondered how they and, more importantly, how I might fare.

I quickly discovered that there was no need to fear for the participants as their enthusiasm to learn was only matched by the speed with which they mastered the subject matter. Indeed, it swiftly became the case that I was doing most of the learning.

The most important lesson to be learnt was that there was a huge and largely ignored thirst for knowledge among citizens that was not being met by conventional education systems. This was all the more impressive because there was a desire for real knowledge rather than the processed variant that exists in an exam-centred second- and third-level education system.

Interestingly, given their ability, the biggest difficulty most of the participants encountered was a lack of confidence. These were women in their forties or older who had left the workforce upon marrying or had not studied at third level; however, they had a wealth of life experience, as well as their own individual talents and abilities, but this did not encourage confidence in them, as it should have. One of the most interesting students in this regard was Christine Buckley, who had not at that time gone public on her own life experiences. I recall being struck at the time by her strength of mind and her innate intelligence but I was also struck by how, at that time, she lacked some critical form of confidence.

While she was a special individual who would have remained in my mind without *Dear Daughter* and all that followed, she was not unique within this class of strong-willed women whom I taught and who taught me.

Throughout the course, she and the rest of the class blossomed (I hope!) to such an extent that I was the one who found myself being stretched to my limits. In this regard, the class became as much of a treat for me as the participants and I found it an exhilarating experience rather than treating it merely as a job. Dundrum provided me with an experience that challenged my preconceptions about age and education.

Too often we believe that education is solely about creating a pathway to work and that it should cease at roughly the age of twenty-five.

****

# Recollection

**Kay O'Reilly**, DATE student, committee member and former treasurer.

I first heard about the classes in September 1984. My son Paul was only one year old at the time and it was marvellous to have the opportunity to get out of the house, to learn something and to know that Paul was being cared for safely.

That first morning I dropped Paul off at the crèche and entered the classroom. I was a bit apprehensive but I need not have worried. I had decided to try Leaving Cert. English but I did not intend to do the exam. I think most people just wanted to do the course but our

English teacher Maura Murphy and the AEO Liam Bane persuaded us otherwise. We really enjoyed the coursework. Maura is an amazing teacher who brought the world of literature to life for us. We duly did our exams and, despite the nerves, we all did very well.

Next term I tackled Leaving Cert. history with Mary Purcell. I thoroughly enjoyed it. I then did economics, followed by French with Jean Swift. I just loved coming to classes. There was such a great atmosphere and great friendships blossomed among the students.

I would particularly like to mention the class 'Law for the Lay Person'. This was a most interesting class with an unusual subject. At the end of term, our tutor took us down to the Four Courts. I am not sure but I think our tutor's father was a barrister. He took us on a conducted tour of the Four Courts and it was a great experience to be given a tour by someone so knowledgeable.

I completed an interior design course before taking on an extramural course from Maynooth College. It was a liberal studies course and our tutor was John Drennan. A fellow student was the late Christine Buckley, that great advocate for children. At the end, we all trooped off to Maynooth to receive our certificates. Following on from that, I completed a literature course at UCD and a psychology course with Nicki O'Leary.

I had come to love DATE, the whole atmosphere, the spirit and the ethos of it. In 1998, I was invited to join the committee and I agreed to do so. I was asked to attend a meeting that night. It turned out to be a planning meeting and I felt a bit lost but committee member Marguerite Thornton came to my rescue.

I have been on the committee ever since and I even did a stint as treasurer in 2006 and 2007. I am still part of DATE after those thirty years. I have learned so much and enjoyed everything. I am so glad that I made that first step all those years ago.

****

Above: Morning in the crèche

Left: Eilish Kavanagh, crèche manager

# Remembering Ann McConnell

**Ann McConnell**, much loved and much missed, was chairperson of DATE from 1986 to 1990, when she was taken from us, still a young woman. She was Ann, the bright spirit of DATE, who became chairperson at a crucial time and who was an inspirational and charismatic leader.

Here, **Daniel McConnell**, Ann's son, and now a political correspondent for the *Sunday Independent*, offers these memories of his mother.

The routine was always the same. We would arrive in from primary school in the late 1980s to see our mum, Ann McConnell, sitting at the kitchen table, doodling. There she would sit, a cup of coffee and a cigarette at the ready, while she drew. Sometimes she would draw on a crisp sheet of A4 paper but more commonly she would just draw on the white surface of our kitchen table. When the table was full, she simply wiped it clean and started again.

The doodles were often dry runs for posters she was readying for a DATE coffee morning, a table quiz or to announce the end of term. Viewing these posters again has brought back so many vivid recollections of her in her element, so happy in what she was doing.

Mum's involvement in DATE became such an important part in her life and I have nothing other than fond memories of that time. As important as her daily pilgrimage to 7.30 a.m. mass was to Mum, DATE was her creative outlet, her social gateway to a wider world outside the four walls of our home. Pauline Brady's Creative Writing class and coffee mornings with Muriel Bolger became the main attractions.

As a mother of six young kids, such respites from her maternal duties meant so much. Samantha, Rebecca, Simon, Adam, Matt and I all fondly remember how much Mum gave to DATE and how much she got back from it in return.

Muriel reminded me recently that back then groups like DATE were few and far between but the crucial role they played in broadening horizons cannot be overstated.

As proud as she was of being a wife to our Dad John and a mother to us, being associated with DATE gave her an identity in her own right. She was Ann the writer, Ann the artist, Ann the friend, Ann the confidant. Not that I realised any of this back then.

But what we certainly did realise was the wonderful group of friends DATE gave her. We had known and loved her huge heart, her infectious laughter and her warm spirit but her character allowed her to thrive at DATE and it was wonderful to see.

DATE was a catalyst for Mum to develop her wonderful creative side. She would go on to win a major prize at the Listowel Writers' Week in 1991. That meant so much to her.

Her friends included great people like Muriel, Pauline, Pamela Uhlemann, Ursula de Brun, Liam Bane, Mary Cummins, Kay Bailey, Mary Elliott, Maura Murphy and many, many others. Our kitchen was regularly filled with their conversation and their friendship. With so many of us, our house was never empty but the kitchen was Mum's centre of operations. Countless cups of coffee were drank, countless cigarettes smoked, countless biscuits eaten, countless tissues used to wipe damp eyes.

During our summer holidays from school, we used to accompany her to DATE when it was located in prefabs at the College of Commerce and also when it was in Taney. We amused ourselves in the playroom for hours as Mum and her pals did their thing and set the world right over their coffees.

But then she stopped going to DATE.

Cancer got in the way and robbed my Mum of her strength and would ultimately rob us of her.

She died in December 1991. I was twelve. My eldest sister Samantha was twenty-one and my youngest brother Matt was just nine. A few short weeks after she died, her wonderful colleagues and friends in DATE organised a mass in her memory in Dundrum church. Despite all the time that has passed, I still remember it vividly. I remember the booklet that was put together. It carried her signature – the same signature found on all her doodles – on the front page.

I remember the tears we all shed that night, adults and children alike. I will never forget the generosity of Mum's pals, particularly Pauline, Ursula and Muriel who gave so much of their time to us after she died.

It is great to see DATE thriving after so many years and to see that some of those familiar names are still involved. Were my mother still here today, I have no doubt she would still be in the thick of it, revelling in the person DATE allowed her to be.

It was once said that a friend is someone who knows you as you are, understands where you have been, accepts what you have become and still allows you to grow. That seems about right.

Prizegiving, with Ann McConnell (on right) with Liam Bane and Kathleen Breathnach

# Popular Art

From the very beginning it was clear that art was going to prove one of the more popular courses on offer at the DATE centre. There was one art class advertised in that first programme and, under the encouraging and cheerful guidance of tutor **Valerie Coombes**, practised artists and aspiring artists sat together and enjoyed the experience. In the second year, the finished works were put on exhibition at the open day. From then on, numbers soared. Ever since, DATE has had a series of top-class art teachers. Now, in September 2014, there are as many as sixteen – yes, sixteen – art classes to choose from and, in addition to the standard watercolours and acrylics and sketching and drawing, there are also courses on the history and appreciation of art and the noble art of calligraphy.

**Beatrice Stewart** has been a supporter of the DATE project from the very start and enrolled as a student in Valerie's art class. She had already gained a diploma in flower arranging and her classes were a regular feature on the programme. An accomplished artist and teacher, as well as a lifelong learner, here are her reflections on her time with DATE.

# Memories of DATE

My involvement with DATE started in 1984. I had been living in Ticknock, Dublin 18, for ten years and, apart from the voluntary work that I was involved with, it seemed that most of my time was spent racing from school to school to collect my four children.

I was attending evening classes, had gained a diploma in flower arranging and was attending the Grafton Academy for tailoring and pattern making. In addition, I had attended a host of other evening classes in a wide variety of disciplines. However, my experience of evening classes was not positive as I felt that the housewife student was viewed as a casual surfer and not to be taken seriously. Most of the time I almost felt like I was a nuisance and the numbers in classes dropped off very quickly. There was not a good atmosphere as everyone, the tutor included, hurried off when class finished, the rooms were cold and draughty and the evening caretakers switched on and off the lights fifteen minutes before the end of class. And I seemed to be the only one that noticed that my classmates' attendance was erratic.

The DATE classes were totally different. The approach here by both the Adult Education Organiser and the voluntary committee was quite clearly intended to encourage adult learners, many of whom had abandoned the world of education, to return and to participate in and enjoy the experience. They were also open to suggestion and so it was that I was taken on initially as a tutor of flower arranging. I loved being involved and passing on the skills that I had acquired. The students were a joy and the committee just made everything run so well. The atmosphere was so life-affirming that I felt reborn.

I joined the counselling class, a two-year certified programme. I went on to complete a third year. DATE had given an opportunity to people who wanted to be involved in the world of education and work. Many of them continued on to Trinity and UCD and graduated. Others became involved with the Rape Crisis Centre while I myself spent eight years as a volunteer with the Samaritans.

The position of art tutor became vacant at DATE and I, having ten years of experience in art, was given the job. I realised then that this was what I really wanted to do. I had found my niche, I loved the job and I was thrilled by the keen interest shown by the students. Through the years, I had doggedly persisted in taking art classes at NCAD and Dún Laoghaire Institute of Art Design and Technology. Having successfully graduated, I went on to UCD where I completed a master's degree, choosing 'Women Artists' as my topic. Throughout this time I continued to be a tutor with DATE. The involvement with both the students and committee was so inspiring and energising that I could not live without it.

My involvement with DATE over thirty years ago has totally changed my life's course. Over the years I have been lucky enough to teach in many places, from church halls to NCAD and IADT, even with FÁS. Gradually I have withdrawn from teaching and college courses. But because of the atmosphere, the one place that I have not given up is the DATE centre. If I stop teaching at DATE, part of me will die. In fact, I hope to be carried out of the premises in a box – but not yet!

****

# Recollection

**Ann O Briain**, student and committee member, writes:

In 1989, with the encouragement of my family, especially my eldest son Dara, I joined the adult education classes in Dundrum. I wanted to believe I had the ability to do my Leaving Cert. English. I, like many of my friends, had left education at fifteen years of age. Now I had more free time. My children were growing up and so I took up the gauntlet and joined Maura Murphy's Leaving Cert. English class.

Maura had a great way of getting each of us to just enjoy the wonder of exploring and learning. Her class was always interesting as I discovered Shakespeare's *Othello*, Patrick Kavanagh and many more poets, dramatists and novelists.

By the time I had got my Leaving Cert. in 1990, I had made many friends and I was proud of my achievements. When the DATE committee asked me to join them, I was delighted. The atmosphere was terrific as people shared their experiences of attending the different classes. In 1991, tragedy struck. Our eldest son Dara died in St Vincent's Hospital after a swift and devastating illness. He was just nineteen years old. Liam and the committee were a lifeline for me then as they encouraged me to remain. I stayed with DATE for the next seven years and went on to enrol in more classes. Psychology was the class that I found most interesting at this time as it taught me to look deeper into myself and helped me to find the strength and courage to carry on. Our wounds still hurt but the scars have healed.

I left DATE to work in occupational therapy in a nursing home for nuns and all the skills I had learned were of great value to me. Sixteen years later I am still working there, nowadays in a part-time capacity. My greatest joy at the home was playing the role of Santa Claus each Christmas, seeing the love and happiness on the faces of the elderly nuns. It was as if they had been transported back to their childhood. When I read to them, they would often compliment me.

Thank you Liam and DATE members, past and present, and thank you to all the fine teachers. It is my privilege to have known you and to have had such wonderful experiences with you.

****

# Remembering Joan Godkin
# (Committee Member 1984–1998)

It was a long-running joke in our house that if there was some kind of job to be done, our mother would be the one doing it. My dad used to swear that Joan Godkin would always end up standing out in the rain, directing cars into the car park or going out for a pint of milk in the snow. But of course the joke was that we all knew she volunteered

Joan Godkin

for those tasks – she probably insisted on doing them. That was why she thrived in her time at DATE, a place where she could work with others who, like her, would step quietly up to the plate and accomplish great things for the community without the need for praise but glad of thanks when it was given.

My sister came across a volunteers' survey that Joan must have filled out some time in the early nineties. So here, in her own words, she articulates the happiness that volunteering in DATE gave her.

*Question 9: What would you see as DATE's greatest success?*
The way it has enriched so many lives. It has helped develop self-confidence and it has helped develop an enormous amount of talent that might otherwise have been dormant.

Joan Godkin and Caitriona Ni Chathain (*muniteoir Ghaeilge*)

*Question 19: Who or what has been your greatest influence since you joined DATE?*
Mary McCarthy who called the first public meeting and 'roped us in' as volunteers. Sadly she died within a couple of years. She showed me how one person, in fact each person, can make a difference to a community when willing to take a chance. She left a wonderful legacy of proof of that.

*If there is anything else that hasn't been covered, please include here:*
I feel the benefits of adult education can have a great influence in a community, not just for the students themselves but their families and friends and it is a pity it is not given more help and recognition. Sometimes I wonder is it that work done by volunteers is not given the same respect as work done by professionals and yet, volunteers can bring a dedication and generosity of time and spirit that can sometimes be lacking in some professionals.

For our family, DATE was a place where my mom could be 'Joan' instead of 'Mammy' and put her skills and enthusiasm to work for the good of others.

**Claire, Sandra and Colette Godkin**

# Bonjour, Buenos Días, Buongiorno, Guten Tag and Conas Atá Tú ...

What began as one French class for beginners in the autumn of 1984 has now, in the autumn programme of 2014, become six French classes, six Italian classes, four Spanish classes, three German classes *agus ceithre ranganna Gaeilge*. A total of twenty-three in all. We have had a number of teachers for the different languages and we are very fortunate that all of them were, and are, top-quality language teachers, as is evident from the scramble for places in these classes year after year. Two of the longest serving are **Yvette O'Leary** and **Kitty O'Sullivan** who are responsible for the ongoing success of the French classes and, as with all of our language teachers, it is thanks to them that students come back, not just to improve their fluency, but to continue to enjoy that special friendly atmosphere that these teachers have created and consistently maintained. Here are Kitty's thoughts on DATE and the French classes:

## The DATE French Classes

During the enrolment period last year, a lady arrived late and expressed an interest in French Beginners. When told the teacher's name, she said with surprise, 'Oh, is that the same Kitty I went to years ago?' When told that it was, she joined the class to begin again. Echoes of Proustian times past ...

Being part of DATE has indeed been a unique and enriching experience for me. It is said that 'teaching is learning' and that applies to teaching adults more than younger people. For some students, classes are a pastime that punctuates the week in wintertime, provided the teacher and homework are fairly easy. However, quite a few have reawakened their enthusiasm and taste for learning and advanced to pastures new.

So what sort of people come to us? One could say 'all sorts of interesting people'. One example is a man called Barney, who is a photographer. He combined his knowledge of written French and photography for a project on the Royal Hospital Kilmainham and this won him a prize in a French competition. He has also cycled extensively in France and recently showed me an example of his camerawork – the bridge from La Rochelle to Île de Ré.

Of course none of these classes would exist if it were not for the dedicated committee members whose tireless efforts behind the scenes and at the coalface keep the wheels in motion. Each year it becomes more evident what a workload it is to set up such a huge number of classes. The committee displays expertise in areas of finance, computer technology and indeed psychology of human resources. Then the other layer of facilitating is provided by Michelle and Aiden. Their efficiency and sense of humour are unmatched. Everything can be 'fixed' or organised by them – for instance, the layout of a classroom can be shifted from computer studies to French class in the blink of an eye.

Let it be known that there has always been a social aspect to DATE, as well as the academic side of things. We have enjoyed gatherings at Christmas, end of school year parties and the official opening of the new location in the town centre, among other things. Again these were the fruits of the committee's efforts. The classes also had a social element. A charming student had her wonderful eightieth birthday celebration, which I was glad to be part of. The venue, I hasten to add, was not the classroom but her son's fine house.

No organisation can function without a chief or team leader. So DATE had, at its inception, the inimitable Liam Bane. It was then a mobile operation so he had to travel between several locations. Since Liam's departure, DATE has been rolling along nicely, headed up by Patricia Doran. Her rather gentle disposition does not prevent her administrative efficiency filtering through to all of us. She has encouraged us in our pursuits.

I can say that my days, years and decades as part of DATE have been happy. There, among teachers and students, I have made good friends and hopefully no enemies.

****

**Concha Gillespie,** a native of Spain, was the star of the Spanish department and a very popular teacher for many years. Here she recounts some of her experiences as a DATE teacher:

# The Spanish Class

I began my job as a DATE teacher in September 1991. The class, Spanish Beginners, was held at the prefab of what is now the College of Further Education in Dundrum. In 1991, the DATE classes were held in six or seven different venues and I can only imagine the inconvenience this must have caused for the organising committee. For me, having taught for many years, the problems always seemed to remain the same in three of these venues. Would I find a space in the car park? Would I be able to carry the books and the radio cassette without dropping anything? And, in one particular location, would I be able to prevent the blackboard from falling on top of some student? The office was in yet another building, which meant a small journey every time photocopying was needed or once a month to claim for payment. Any annoyance this could have caused was immediately assuaged by the secretary Celia and, later on, Berni with their helpfulness and good humour. You always left the place feeling like a better person.

What about the students? They came to DATE to learn Spanish for different reasons – some had learnt it at school or university and wanted to refresh or improve their knowledge, quite a few had sons or daughters living in Spain and wanted to communicate with their Spanish grandchildren, while others went to Spain on holiday and some just wanted to learn a new language and culture. As we struggled together in a relaxed atmosphere with lots of banter as well as serious discussion about grammar, history and even politics, we learned from one another. I learned, for example, that a language can be mastered at any age. In that respect, I particularly remember a student who came as a beginner and went on to have a great command of the language using words that I had forgotten. He used to watch the Spanish news every evening, recording the programme and watching it again at breakfast time and at lunch time the following day. Many other students also attained high levels of proficiency without having had any previous knowledge of the language. There was a great bond among students and some became very good friends. They helped each other and also came to my rescue when I was in need of help.

There would, of course, have been no students or classes without the committee. While they organised the classes, served refreshments and looked after things generally, it is their kindness that I remember most – not only to me but to every student. We were all treated with such respect and given a warm welcome. They really cared. And in addition, the fact that it is a totally voluntary group of people makes it one of those miracles of life that cheer you up when you are tempted to lose faith in humanity.

When we finally got our premises in the Dundrum Town Centre, all my problems with parking, carrying loads and handing in forms were instantly resolved. The office was now beside the classrooms and

Michelle always very kindly reminded us to give her the claims form and Aiden really looked after my cassette and CD player and any other objects that I might leave behind. My life became easier and, rightly or wrongly, I took it as a reward in my older years.

John O'Callaghan and Yvette O'Laoire

Maureen Nolan, Concha Gillespie, Mary Sarsfield, Eileen O'Brien

**Mary Madigan** writes of her experiences as a student of the French language at DATE.

# Thirty Years a-DATE-ing

I was first introduced to Dundrum Adult Training and Education when I picked up one of the brochures advertising the DATE autumn schedule of classes in the early 1990s.

I joined the DATE Beginners French class under the watchful instruction of Kitty O'Sullivan. From day one, it required a real commitment – we had to learn a comprehensive vocabulary, understand the idiosyncrasies of the French language and grammar, read and discuss the particular book selected for study and be aware of what was happening in contemporary France.

There were, however, some 'out of class' events – for instance, I remember fondly a five-day trip to Paris organised by a group of the 1998 class. It was my first trip to Paris and the many places we visited there made the trip unforgettable. I can still recall staring in awe at the Vincent Van Gogh painting *The Starry Night* in the Musée d'Orsay – what a magical memory. Another highlight was our visit to the Musée de l'Orangerie where we saw Claude Monet's *Les Nymphéas* – truly stunning.

After a few years, I graduated to the next level and found myself under the guidance of the ever-enthusiastic Yvette O Laoire. Now, I was attending two classes a week: the Monday class was more concerned with the study of grammar and books while the Friday was more centred around conversation.

Among the many books we studied were Marcel Pagnol's *Manon des Sources* and Pierre Peju's *La petite Chartreuse*. They gave us an insight into the historical and cultural background of France and its people. In the conversation classes, the discussion would encompass the latest happenings in France, the EU or indeed the wider world.

About three years ago, Emilie Champenois joined the teaching staff, taking charge of the Monday classes. This year, after Yvette's retirement, Emilie took charge of the Friday class, bringing her own particular enthusiasm, style and approach to her classes.

What I have particularly enjoyed in the DATE adult education programme is the opportunity to learn in a very engaging environment, where the teacher is fully supportive of the students and encourages everyone to participate and where the friendships, developed over the years, endure and flourish.

I believe that, by returning to the classes each year, while continuing to study the new programme set for the year, the students are able to practise what they have learned in previous years so that, when spending time in France or another country where French is spoken, the opportunity is there to think and converse continuously in French. There is a very apt French proverb that describes this process – *c'est en forgeant qu'on devient forgeron* – which means 'practice makes perfect'.

By participating in such classes, thinking and speaking in French becomes second nature so that it is possible to carry on an everyday conversation with native speakers. This is evident when listening to the various students recounting their trips to France and their ability to engage in conversation regarding everyday matters without difficulty. I have also found myself able to converse with French visitors to Ireland in Dublin, Clare and Connemara – all thanks to the DATE French classes.

*Bien sûr je suis très fière d'avoir assisté aux courses de français organisés par le DATE.* (Yes, I am proud to have attended the French classes organised by DATE.) I would like to pay the warmest possible tribute to all those who have served on the DATE committee for the selfless work they do to provide such opportunities to those interested in the myriad of subjects available.

*Je souhaite vivement que la comité poursuive son travail dans cette voie et je voudrais féliciter toute la comité pour son engagement et ses accomplissements pour le bien de la communauté depuis ces trentes dernières années de service excellent.* (I would urge the committee to continue its work and I would like to congratulate all of the committee for all that it has accomplished during thirty years of excellent service for the good of the community.) *Acceptez, je vous prie, mes très sincères remerciements.* (Please accept my sincere thanks.) *Bien amicalement.*

****

Bhí – agus tá – ana shuim freisin i bhfoghlaim na Gaeilge a bhí le faíl i rith an treimhse seo – ranganna a raibh ainmeacha éagsula orthu, mar shampla, Cúpla Focail, Bígí ag Labhairt agus go simplí, Gaeilge. Is í **Maire Mhic Gearailt** atá i mbun cursaí faoi láthair. Múinteoir den scoth is ea Máire and seo í ag cur síos ar na ranganna.

# Gaeilge i nDún Droma

Thosaigh mé ag múineadh Gaeilge do dhaoine fásta anseo i nDún Droma sa bhliain 2004 i bhfoirgneamh réamh dhéanta in aice leis an 'College of Further Education' ar an bpríomhshráid. Chuir sé gliondar chroí orm an méad daoine a bhí ag foghalim na Gaeilge a fheiceáil agus ó shin i Leith tá líon na micléinn ag dul ó neart go neart. Sa bhliain 2006 bhogamar ar aghaidh go dtí an Ionad Siopadóireachta anseo agus táimid go léir an shásta leis an áit ghalánta seo agus na háiseanna nua-aimseartha atá ar fáil dúinn ar an gcúigiú leibhéal. Buailimid le chéile dhá uair sa tseachtain, dhá rang ar an Déardaoin agus dá rang eile ar an Aoine. Tá meascán maith idir dhaoine óga agus daoine níos sine, idir náisiúntachtí eile ague Éireannaigh agus tuismitheoirí le páistí óga agus déagoirí atá ag freastal ar scoileanna éagsúla agus daoine atá ar scor. Réitíonn gach éinne go hiontach le chéile agus bíonn an sport agus spraoi again i rith na ranganna. Éiríonn an tsuim atá ag daoine sa Ghaeilge de réir a chéile agus tagann ardú meanman orm nuair a fheicim go bhfuil na daoine i bhfad níos bródúla as a dteanga agus a gcultúr Gaelach sa lá inniu ann. Is iontach an mhaise é go bhfuil said ag freastal ar ranganna mar seo agus go bhfuil said toilteannach an Ghaeilge a thabhairt ar aghaidh don chéad ghliún eile. Dar lion is mór an phríbhléid domsa bheith ábalta cabhrú leis na daoine ár dteanga agus ár noidhreacht a choimeád beo agus go háirithe i dtimpeallacht atá suimhneach agus in atmaisféar greannmhar. Táimid go léir ag déanamh ár seacht ndícheall chun cloí chomh fada agus is féidir leis an ráiteas seo leanas a scríobh Iar Uachtarán na hÉireann Pádraig Ó hIrghíle sa bhlian 1982.

Na lig don teanga bás a fháil an fhad a bheidh sibh beo, labhair í agus tabhair í mar oidhreacht don aos óg, ná bíodh sé ar bhur gconsais gur sibh a chaill an tseoid.

# Health
# and Fitness

From the very beginning health and fitness classes have been a regular feature of the DATE educational programme. There have always been classes in yoga and its related diverse forms, including reflexology and tai chi. **Patricia Crimin** is one of a number of excellent yoga teachers that have been employed by DATE over the years. In this piece she describes the benefits which so many students have derived from their attendance at the DATE yoga classes.

## The Joys of Yoga

As we are celebrating thirty years of DATE, it is interesting to note that yoga has always been a special part of the education programme. It was one of the first classes on offer back in the beginning, thanks to the vision of the wonderful committee who founded DATE. Over the years, yoga has maintained its popularity and now there are three classes a week, catering for about sixty people. Some of the students in their eighties have been doing yoga for longer than their teacher and are a fantastic source of inspiration for her!

Yoga has taken place in different venues with a host of wonderful teachers over the years. Classes are now held in the lovely Dom

Marmion Centre under the direction of Patricia Crimin, YTI teacher and therapist.

Did you know that yoga has been around for over 5,000 years? So what is yoga? Yoga is a scientific system that combines postures (exercises), breathing techniques, relaxation and meditation along with moral and spiritual principles (it is not a religion).

The DATE brochure invites you to come and explore the many benefits of hatha yoga so, if you haven't done so already, there is no ailment that will prevent you from giving it a go! The classes begin with sitting in a chair doing relaxing breathing, then we move on to gentle warm-ups before exploring different postures to help strengthen and stretch each part of the body, with everybody going at their own pace. As yoga is so closely linked to nature, it's a real pleasure on warm days when the class gets the opportunity to experience some time outdoors in the beautiful garden at the Dom Marmion centre, becoming aware of the sunshine or a breeze on your skin while being serenaded by birdsong!

Yoga has something wonderful to offer everyone, regardless of age, creed or physical abilities, so long as we are open to adapting and content to go at a pace that is suitable for us at the different stages of our life. Over my years of teaching yoga at DATE, some of the classes have been greatly improved. Wheelchair users have been integrated into the class where participants range from beginners to well-seasoned yogis and exercise alongside those who are living with arthritis and other such difficulties so that all can work safely together at their own level in a gentle, supportive and compassionate environment that creates a Sacred Space of Tender Loving Care.

Through various combinations of practices determined by personal needs and abilities, it has been proved that yoga can help to improve physical and mental health and happiness as it brings about a wonderful sense of well-being and harmony of mind, body and spirit.

Mindfulness has become a buzz word recently. It is the practice of purposely focusing our attention on the present moment and accepting it without judgement. Yoga is a mindfulness practice as it helps to keep us 'grounded in the moment', allowing us to go on a personal journey of discovery to see more clearly what is going on inside our mind, body and emotions.

Teaching yoga with DATE, I've come to realise that while the class may appear a bit isolated as it takes place in a building away from most of the other classes, there is a great sense of being part of a community – and that is a wonderful feeling … This is especially evident at enrolment times. Many of the course teachers help the committee at this busy time. For me, it's a lovely time to reconnect with those I haven't seen during long holiday breaks and it also gives me the opportunity to chat and welcome new people into the yoga circle. Namaste!

\*\*\*\*

# Recollection

**Ann Brodie** is a member and former chairperson of the DATE committee.

To the best of my recollection, I joined DATE in 2000. Having retired in 1999, I had enrolled for a class and was very impressed by the process and the atmosphere. Some time later, I came across a notice stating they were looking for extra volunteers. My background was in education so after a chance meeting with a member of the committee, I expressed my willingness to become involved. Later I was invited to help with the provision of teas and coffees for the DATE students in rather primitive surroundings. Eventually I was invited to join the committee.

After I became the honorary secretary, DATE organised an art exhibition, prompted by the urgings and assistance of students. It wouldn't have been possible without the work and co-operation of Teresa O'Neill, who was an innovative chairperson. We also had the privilege of visiting President Mary McAleese in Áras an Uachtaráin.

In 2005, shortly after I had been elected chairperson, we finally took possession of our present premises in Dundrum Town Centre. Kathleen Walker had been the driving force behind acquiring this great facility. The task of moving was daunting as it involved the transfer of records, books, equipment and furniture from various venues in Dundrum. It demanded complex teamwork, not only from the committee members but also from spouses and other family members. Most of the transfer work had to be carried out at night due to the regulations of the DTC. We also had the wonderful help and co-operation of our AEO Patricia Doran who moved as quickly as possible to appoint a caretaker. Later when our part-time secretary was appointed to a full-time position with the VEC, Patricia was very prompt in appointing a replacement.

The next few years saw another art exhibition opened by the late Minister for the Arts, Seamus Brennan, and the official opening of the centre by Junior Minister Sean Haughey. Our tea room has been very successful in its objective to allow students to mix socially outside the classroom.

I was honoured to take on the office of chairperson but thankful to be free of its onerous duties. I feel privileged to have worked with Dolores Byrne, Eileen O'Brien and Roisin Daly.

****

Presentation: Mary Elliott, Mary Banotti MEP, Olive Carroll; (seated) Marguerite Thornton, Kay Bailey

Presentation: Celia Gaffney, Dolores Byrne, Eileen O'Brien, Teresa O'Neill, Marguerite Thornton, Kay Bailey

# Leisure Time Activities

Needless to say, there were many who came to DATE looking for classes which did not require the intensity or pressure of studying for examinations and certificates. Their preferred option was classes that did not make too many demands and in which they could participate and learn 'at their own chosen speed'. Such classes as philosophy, music and art appreciation, calligraphy, gardening, digital camera and others were always popular and well attended over the years. Most popular of all in this department was bridge and a great host of enthusiasts gathered at the Dom Marmion Centre for the classes, which later became the Club.

**Mary O'Brien**, committee member and bridge player, here writes about the pleasure that people derived from these bridge classes, which were led by the late lamented Phyllis Rutherford.

## The Bridge Club

The stereotypical vision people have of bridge – columns of cigar smoke curling up to a low hung lamp – is very far from the scene in Dom Marmion Hall every Wednesday morning.

The DATE bridge club is a very mixed group – mostly homemakers, pensioners, 'ladies who lunch'. Many believe the club has enriched their lives. Many of the attendees might otherwise have been experiencing loneliness, especially those who have suffered a bereavement. In the playing of bridge, there is a sense of achievement when the 'contract' is made. It is a fascinating game, an intellectual pastime where there is no stake and everything boils down to a contest of wills.

The Club was established by Phyllis Rutherford who believed that it was never too late or too early to learn the intricacies of bridge. Phyllis's contribution has been so much more than expertise as her patience and attention to detail were invaluable. She treated every member of the Club with courtesy and respect. Her advice, especially to new members, was, 'If you can't play well, play fast and enjoy the game – and be polite and friendly with opponents.'

Our saddest day was when we attended Phyllis's funeral. She will never be forgotten. Her spirit lives on in the Club where the members are more interested in the well-being of their colleagues than in reaching the dizzy heights of championship bridge.

It would be difficult to describe the hours of pleasure we have enjoyed in the Club. Recently, we celebrated the birth of triplet grandchildren to one of our members.

The club is now in the safe hands of Seamus Morgan, our hardworking tournament director, who is only too happy to give a ruling on any apparent irregularity.

There is no A team or B team – just players who want to spend some quality time with their friends and enjoy a cup of tea at the break.

****

Other activities enjoyed over the years include Reading Circles and Public Speaking.

**Phil Dunne** has a long association with DATE both as a student and a teacher. In this piece, Phil reflects on those DATE years.

# Learning and Teaching at DATE

I first heard of DATE when my late husband joined a creative writing class in 1985. A year or so later, I joined a yoga class in the old Taney School. The class was held at 9.30 a.m. on Monday mornings. Lying on the floor with a draught coming in under the door and the heating system slowly cranking up, I felt sure the cold would drive me away. However, little did I know that this would be the start of a long association with DATE. Funnily enough, it would always be on a Monday morning. In September 1987, Liam rang me saying that the committee was thinking of offering a Public Speaking class and he asked if I would like to act as tutor. My husband had died suddenly earlier that year and though still in a somewhat shell-shocked state, I said yes.

The class started that September in a small prefab room on the grounds of the VEC College in Dundrum. The room was totally unsuitable for a public speaking class as a thin partition wall was all that separated us from the adjoining room and the crèche was much too close. I wondered how could I encourage people with no experience of public speaking to have the courage to find their voices. Those were obvious challenges but there were other compensating factors. Firstly, there was the wonderful voluntary committee. Walking in the door of the prefab, the first thing one saw was a large table with two cheerful volunteers serving tea and biscuits. Around this always crowded space, views were exchanged, friendships formed and support given.

## Public Speaking

Most of the students attending those first public speaking classes were women thinking of returning to the workforce. There were only a few men. The motivation was often to serve their communities better whether on a parent/teacher association, a residents' group or a golf committee. The single class quickly became two classes, beginners and intermediate. It was wonderful to see the confidence and ability of the students increase, realising of course that this increased confidence was as much due to their fellow class members as it was to me.

One year our class was enlivened by the arrival of two students from St Benildus College who attended as part of their transition year. One of those two boys, who went on to become an actor and writer, presented the first argument in favour of the legalisation of cannabis that most of the class had ever heard. Quickly the class became much more than a public speaking venue as people spoke of their hopes, commitments and passions more and more. My mind was opened as I heard members of the Jewish and Bahá'í faiths share their beliefs, as well as parents expressing their wish to integrate their physically and mentally handicapped children into mainstream education. One of the most common aims for people was to be able to ask questions at public meetings. We spent a lot of class time practising the art of questioning with the inevitable result that students found themselves on committees where they would continue to question and probe.

As the nineties ended, the public speaking class seemed to come to a natural end. I think this was partly because, in a time of full employment, the class was composed mainly of retired people who had other interests. By this time, although I was working in other areas with the South Co. Dublin Adult Education Service, I had no wish to end my connection with DATE.

## The Reading Circle

Liam came up with the title for my next class – the Reading Circle. This class started over ten years ago (on Mondays of course!) and has given me and, I hope, the students great enjoyment. In part, like a book club, we read books of fiction and non-fiction but, as we meet weekly, the book is discussed in-depth on a week-by-week basis as we read. Poetry forms an important part of the class and we usually study a particular poet or movement for a term. We also read plays, often one that is being performed at a Dublin theatre during the term. A novel, poetry and a play seems a lot to fit in to a one-and-half-hour class but we seem to manage it, as well as allowing people to share their opinions on whatever we're studying.

Over the years, we have had wonderful readings and performances (in the Kilternan centre) on themes connected with our reading. Some of the most memorable for me have been a reading by the contemporary Irish poet Paula Meehan in 2009 and the actors and writers Donal O'Kelly and Sorcha Fox performing extracts from the play *Cambria* after we had read *Narrative of Frederick Douglass, an American Slave* in 2011. Another delightful performance was *Songs of Joyce*, based on songs from *Dubliners*.

When DATE finally moved into the long-promised purpose-built adult education centre in 2006, we all wondered if it would be possible to keep the spirit of DATE alive. Our fears were groundless, thankfully. DATE continues to thrive in its new venue, committee members are still on hand and students attend in even larger numbers. I continue to be amused that I go to work in a shopping centre but it has advantages. Parking is never a problem, we have a selection of venues for our end-of-term lunches while the LUAS has added a whole new catchment area for students.

What is very clear thirty years on is that the vision, commitment and hard work of the voluntary committee have borne fruit beyond anyone's dreams. It's impossible to say what the next thirty years will bring but it will surely be beyond what can be imagined today.

You're looking good! – Dolores Byrne, Maureen Flynn, Elma Murray, Katherine Chandler

Happy Birthday Fionn!

# A Decade of DATE
## 2004-2014

**Patricia Doran** has been the Adult Education Officer with Dublin and Dún Laoghaire Adult Education and Training Board since 2004. She oversaw the transition to the new premises and ensured that the DATE operation was secured and would continue to deliver the same first-class service over the following ten years.

Almost midway through the second decade of the twenty-first century, the DATE phenomenon celebrates thirty years in operation. In the role of Adult Education Officer, I am proud of my association with this programme. The DATE classes owe their success and continuation to the voluntary committee over many years, my predecessor Liam Bane, the tutors, a long line of secretaries and the women who staffed the crèche.

Since November 2006, Aiden Gallagher has become synonymous with the adult education centre in Dundrum Town Centre. All agree that his work has been an essential support to the committee, the tutors and the students.

## Tutors and Committee

One cannot underestimate the role of the tutors. They have delivered the classes and ensured that high standards have been maintained.

Their success is illustrated by the level of repeat custom over a long period of time. On the occasions when I have had the opportunity to visit classes, I always have a yearning to stay and participate. Some tutors have retired over this period and are missed very much by all – Roisin O'Donnell, Maria (Concha) Gillespie and most recently Yvette O Laoire and Maura Murphy. Sadly, George Ferguson passed away. It is as if the term *gentleman and scholar* was coined especially to describe this elegant man.

Of course, I had known about DATE, encountered their work and met some of the DATE committee members before I took up the role of Adult Education Officer in 2004. At the head office of Co. Dublin VEC, the DATE committee members were recognised as 'a formidable group of women'. This is a recognition of the volunteerism that is rooted in the community and focussed on action. It takes account of the needs of women but does not exclude men, as DATE made clear from the beginning with the inclusion of the late John O'Callaghan as a member of the committee. This group has worked in collaboration with Co. Dublin VEC (now Dublin Dún Laoghaire Education Training Board) and has contributed to the development of so many individuals through the provision of classes for adults.

In conversation with DATE committee members, it is apparent that their engagement with this unique story has formed a vital part of their own story. I have spoken about the manner in which it has enhanced their assertiveness, given them greater confidence in their own abilities and brought them to a realisation of the power in each individual as well as how the collective can work together to achieve its aims. This aura of confidence must surely be felt by the students who attend the classes. There have been changes in membership over the years and my own memory is of the former treasurer, the late Sheena Price, whom I will always remember as a feisty lady with a ready sense of humour.

In September 2004 I was a new Adult Education Officer learning the scope of the many strands of the South Dublin Adult Education Service. The DATE programme consisted of a wide range of approximately sixty classes. One could say they were literally 'all over the place'. Classes were held in the prefab at the College of Further Education in Dundrum, the Holy Cross primary school, Dom Marmion Hall, Taney Parish Centre and Airfield Estate. In my very first week in office, I had received an invitation to a meeting with Teresa O'Neill, then chairperson of DATE. There was possibly a certain level of trepidation as we all met for the first time in our respective roles. My recollection is that it did not take too many encounters before we all warmed to each other and I enjoyed being a part of the camaraderie so obvious among the group. At that time the meetings were held in the evenings at 1B Ballinteer Road. After 2006, when these meetings were no longer necessary, I missed those evenings.

## A New Beginning

September 2006 heralded a new beginning for the DATE programme. The new Dundrum Town Centre was to incorporate community facilities, thanks to the efforts of DATE and to Mary Elliott and Kathleen Walker in particular. The project was supported enthusiastically by Co. Dublin VEC and developed as a three-way partnership consisting of a statutory body, private industry and the voluntary group DATE. This project and the inclusion of DATE would not have been possible without the support of Co. Dublin VEC. Mary Elliott played a pivotal role at this time and the openness of the former Education Officer, Fiona Hartley, has to be acknowledged as has the support of the CEO, Pat O'Connor. There were trips in high-visibility jackets and hard hats to the building site and negotiations and many meetings with Phil Reilly, representing Glenrye Properties Services Ltd., over a period of two years before the big move into the new premises could be realised in September 2006.

Even positive change creates its own difficulties. Ann Brodie had taken up the role of DATE chairperson at this challenging time. Because of the nature of the location, much of the moving and organisation had to happen at night. On one of the most onerous nights, when Shane McGovern of the Town Centre was assisting me, members of the DATE committee arrived to check if I needed help. I was most heartened by the warmth of their support on that evening and the clear communication between myself and Ann Brodie over this period.

Berni Fitzpatrick was there to support and assist with settling in but it was November before Aiden Gallagher commenced as caretaker. The fully operational centre took on a different dimension in terms of the care and attention it needed. Berni and Aiden, in their respective roles, worked together to ensure success and support for all. When Berni was promoted later, Michelle Kelly stepped into the role and made it her own. The social element of the classes, which is very important, continued with the bright new kitchen organised by the DATE committee. The Dom Marmion Centre was still retained as a venue.

## Progress All the Way ...

It was progress all the way over the next few years and decisions had to be made regarding organisational change, especially in relation to enrolling. In 2007, the computer room was fully equipped and an art exhibition showcased the work of students attending DATE's many art classes. DATE, part of the South Dublin Adult Education Services 'Celebration of Learning and Partnership', was launched by the former minister of state, Sean Haughey, in 2008. This put the focus on something positive at the onset of a grim socio-economic reality, which we hope is coming to an end. The event was supported generously by Dundrum Town Centre Management and especially Don Nugent, the director. There was recognition that the DATE classes and other adult education classes provided a bridge between the community and the Town Centre. Of course they have also increased the general footfall, which is good for business.

By the time Dolores Byrne became chairperson, it was time to change from the giant yellow registers to a new computerised system.

Patricia Doran AEO, Fionn Doyle, Eileen O'Brien, Felicity Fitzpatrick

Led by Dolores, the DATE volunteers learned the system in order to input the enrolment data. Perhaps when the systems are fully developed, online enrolment will become common. Eileen O'Brien took on the role of chairperson in the year of unprecedented weather conditions, including floods and arctic snows.

Since its inception in 1984, the classes themselves have been the central focus of DATE and there has always been a great willingness to embrace change. At one time the accredited programmes such as the Junior and Leaving Certificate were an important part of the overall delivery. Extramural certification through Maynooth College and UCD also featured for a period. Now new subjects have been introduced. The most recent is an Introduction to Chinese Culture with Mandarin. Keeping pace with the needs of the community in terms of adult education must remain a feature of any programme and those who deliver it. The ability to attract new members and incorporate change has been a major factor in the success of DATE over three decades. One of the great challenges of the future for any group will be to ensure the relevance of the classes offered to our ever-changing society.

The period 2004–2014 has been a period of development and consolidation. The current chairperson Roisin Daly will have new challenges to face going forward and I wish the new chairperson and the committee every success in that endeavour. I have not named the DATE committee members who have worked so hard to ensure the success of this programme but I hope this publication will give recognition to their dedication over the years. I am sure you will all agree that DATE is a vital part of the fabric of life in Dundrum and the surrounding area.

Roisin Daly, Chairperson

# Celebrating Thirty Years of DATE

It is fitting that the final contribution should come from **Roisin Daly**, the current chairperson of DATE.

In 2005 when Dundrum Town Centre first opened, I and many others were looking forward to the country's biggest ever indoor shopping centre. We were promised numerous shops, cafés, bars over four floors in a state-of-the-art building. Over the following three years, more than 70 million people would visit the centre.

But on the fifth floor things were very different. Adult education, community services and studios for radio broadcasting were located here. The world inside the doors on this floor contrasted strongly with the floors beneath. The hustle and bustle of shoppers below, many of them unaware of this fifth floor, were replaced by a learning and social environment. DATE, in co-operation with Dublin and Dún Laoghaire ETB, offers a broad range of adult daytime classes including various languages, art, classical studies, philosophy, computers for fun, history, crafts, enjoying English in its many forms and many others.

DATE, now celebrating its thirtieth year in the Dundrum area, the last eight of these in the Dundrum Town Centre, is run by a voluntary committee of dedicated people who have given and continue to give their time freely to help further the needs of adult education and lifelong learning. I like the idea of daytime classes, of meeting new people and, yes, shopping in this amazing new centre. The atmosphere during enrolment for classes was buzzing with excitement and enthusiasm for the months ahead. Each new term at DATE is a great opportunity for students to meet like-minded people and to forge friendships and relationships with other students, which leads to a more active social life for many and is of tangible benefit to the community. The emphasis here, which is very obvious to everyone, especially the students, is on enjoyment and having fun while learning.

DATE represents a new beginning for many, including me. I enjoyed my chosen classes so much that I joined this group of volunteers to help them in their work providing such classes. The 'chat room' at DATE is the drop-in tea room where students, tutors and others can meet, relax, exchange ideas and chat over a cup of tea before or after a class. This in itself helps all to keep abreast of what is happening in the world of learning. Each new term, anxious and keen to secure a place, students will queue from early morning on enrolling days. This year I met a group of five or six students enrolling for their twenty-fourth year in a language class. That has to be a record!

2014 sees DATE celebrating thirty years of teaching and learning. I applaud this and congratulate the current committee and previous committees who, with the support of DDLETB, have made this lifelong learning establishment in Dundrum so valuable and accessible to those who wish to continue to enrich their lives with learning.

I wish them many more years of success in providing this service. Lifelong learners in today's fast-changing world are a valuable asset to all of society thanks to their unique life experiences and skills.

Lifelong learning is for all ages. Education sets us free.